Sugar & Salt

My Life with Bipolar Disorder

by
Jane Thompson

Bloomington, IN  Milton Keynes, UK

AuthorHouse™
1663 Liberty Drive, Suite 200
Bloomington, IN 47403
www.authorhouse.com
Phone: 1-800-839-8640

AuthorHouse™ UK Ltd.
500 Avebury Boulevard
Central Milton Keynes, MK9 2BE
www.authorhouse.co.uk
Phone: 08001974150

First published by AuthorHouse 8/9/2006

ISBN: 1-4259-5317-4 (sc)

Library of Congress Control Number: 2006906853

Printed in the United States of America
Bloomington, Indiana

This book is printed on acid-free paper.

Dedicated to:

George, Mary Jo, and Betsy

ACKNOWLEDGEMENTS

I need to thank my doctors. Without them, I would not have the quality of life I have now, and there is a good chance I would not be alive at all. Dr. Gary Kula diagnosed me and got me over the hard part of realizing and accepting that I had a mental illness. He did therapy with me and helped me understand my situation. Dr. James Shupe truly listened and understood. He prescribed the first medication that was really effective for me and gave me confidence that I could get better. Dr. Rudy Molina worked unflappably with me through the crises of a medication change, the loss of a job and my home. Dr. Stuart Crane helped me through the vagaries of applying for disability insurance, and my current doctor, Kerrie Halfant, has been unfailingly helpful and supportive. I have had other doctors and, almost without exception, they have refused to listen to me, have prescribed medication that they thought I should take without really consulting me, and have simply given up when their therapies haven't worked. I shall not mention their names.

I wish to thank all my Mensa friends who supported me in my writing career, cheering me on as I took baby steps toward it. I especially include my Mensa editors, and the late Bailey Hankins, who saw talent where little was evident. Wayne Pierce has always been there for me; even during dark times

I also thank those who are closest to me and without whose encouragement this book could not have been written. These include especially Bruce Belland, my writing buddy, and Penny Jo Lynch. Mary Jo Casey read and reread the book while it was being written without complaint. A special thanks to Tracey Bryn Belland, of Voice of the Beehive, who allowed me to use her fantastic lyrics in the book, and to Roger

Durham, who contributed the Forward.

Jane Thompson

Georgetown, Texas

June, 2006

jtokc@yahoo.com

Monsters and Angels

I'm nobody's wife, and I'm nobody's baby
I like it that way, but then again...maybe.
I'm nobody's Valentine and I'm nobody's pearl,
When you get it right down to it, what I always seem to find...
Is just some girl singing,

There are monsters there are angels,
there's a peacefulness and a rage inside us all
there is sugar and there is salt;
there is ice and there is fire, in every single heart
there are monsters. there are angels.

I'm nobody's promise and I'm nobody's chore
and I ain't got nobody that I feel I gotta
live for...nobody to live for
I'm nobody's work and I'm nobody's company
every time I turn around I always seem to find
just me....singing

There are monsters there are angels,
there's a peacefulness and a rage inside us all
there is sugar and there is salt
there is ice and there is fire, in every single heart
there are monsters, there are angels.

I'm nobody's wife and I'm nobody's baby
I like it that way, but then again...maybe
(then again, maybe)
I'm nobody's Valentine and I'm nobody's pearl,
When you get it right down to it, what I always seem to find...
Is just some girl singing

There are monsters there are angels,
there's a peacefulness and a rage inside us all
there is sugar and there is salt

there is ice and there is fire, in every single heart
there are monsters. there are angels.

singing there are monsters there are angels
singing there are monsters there are angels
(I'm nobody's wife)
singing there are monsters there are angels
(and I'm nobody's baby)
singing there are monsters there are angels
(I'm nobody's mother)
singing there are monsters there are angels
(and I'm nobody's child)

Tracey Bryn Belland
1991
Honey Lingers
Voice of the Beehive
used with permission

FOREWARD

At first glance, this book may appear to be nothing more than a series of entertaining anecdotes. It is that, of course, but on closer inspection it also turns out to contain a fascinating glimpse into the life of a very private person. With consummate skill and meticulous candor, Jane Thompson has revealed the essence of an individual whose existence a quarter-century of friendship never led me to suspect.

From rural Oklahoma to the boulevards of suburban Dallas, Jane leads the reader gently through the minefields of her life with her own unique blend of wry humor, courage, determination, and disillusionment. Jane has been down, but she's never been out, and her stories illustrate the eternal values of perseverance, self-reliance, and unflinching honesty. If she has a fault, it is only that she has hidden her inmost thoughts from the world far too well, and for far too long.

In these stories, collected here for the first time, we see a real person, dealing with real problems and real frustrations, and frequently succeeding through sheer "cussedness", as Jane's Oklahoma kinfolk would undoubtedly put it. Better acquainted with adversity than fortune, Jane deftly spins her tales with a light touch that belies the heartfelt emotion underlying these experiences. Let's hope the present volume is only the first of many.

Roger Durham
June, 2006

INTRODUCTION

When I hung up the phone, I knew it was over. And I had sworn this was the last one. Actually, this one sneaked in under the radar. I had always had problems with relationships and had given up on having a successful one. This guy spent six weeks wining and dining me, sending me flowers and convincing me with his sensitivity that he was the one I could trust. I played, no hell, I didn't play, I *was* hard to get until after weeks of testing him, I realized that if I got breast cancer , this dude wouldn't run out on me. He knew my big secret, and that hadn't scared him. He loved my cats, missed me when I was out of town, and had seen me and didn't flinch right after I woke up. He thought I looked great just as I was and insisted I was a talented writer. A real keeper.

His name was Mark. He'd come over in the middle of the week, then take me out for breakfast in the morning just because he couldn't wait until the weekend to see me. The cat would sleep on his shirt and get cat hair all over it, and he would just laugh. On top of all his other good features, he was good-looking.. He was funny and wanted to know all about me.

Just after I made the decision that I was *in love* with him, he didn't show up for a Saturday date and I didn't hear from him all weekend. Now that set off some alarm bells; when I did not hear from him on Monday, I just had to know what was going on. So I called him up. "What happened?" was all I said (by this time he recognized my voice on the telephone without any other identification). After all, you do have to assume that something big at work or home came up; but then, of course, you still wonder why you didn't get a phone call. His answer? A simple one: "I'm seeing someone else." I just hung up the phone. I knew all I needed to know. I was flabbergasted. I couldn't even figure out how he had time to even think of someone else -- I hadn't had a clue. And now, so suddenly, he was finished with me. After getting so close to me, convincing me that he really cared about me, he was done. And I had just started.

I was blind with fury and regret. Did he really think that he could stop paying attention to me with no consequences? Did he think that he could just forget me? That I would go away quietly? How could he just dump me with no regard to my feelings or my future? Well, he couldn't. All I could think about was how I felt and how I wanted him to pay attention to me. I wanted to be the most important thing in his life. My mind was blank except for that one thought. The feelings were overwhelming; the urge to do something to relieve those feelings was overpowering.

The only thing is, that didn't happen. The suicide, I mean. The rest happened. I'm bipolar, or manic-depressive, but I'm stable on medication. After I hung up the phone, I felt a lot of the same things I described. And I cried. And I wrote a poem. That's all.

ROMANCE 101

Ultimately, reluctantly, I trusted this new love.

He brought flowers, gentle humor, generous affection and hope.

I wept when I found he was just killing time;

And learned, once more,

Not to trust.

But I do know how people who are not on medication or who have not been diagnosed properly can do outrageous things. Fifteen percent[1] of people with bipolar disorder kill themselves. Rarely, they hurt or kill people. I know what it feels like and I've been there.

---

[1] 1 Fawcett, J., Golden, B., & Rosenfeld, N. (2000). *New Hope for People with Bipolar Disorder*, **p. 136**

Chapter 1: I'm Nobody's Wife

The first time I can remember being depressed was when I was seven. It was a result of family Christmas traditions. Christmas always smelled special. It was a distinct time of the year. We didn't have to hold our breaths, fearing what would happen next. It was the only time of the year when our lives were predictable.

My mother had six brothers and sisters, and so did my father. We had loving aunts and uncles on both sides, and cousins galore. For Christmas each year, my mother baked for our relatives and friends. The house smelled wonderful for weeks. My father sat on the kitchen steps, day in and day out, cracking pecans with an old-fashioned nutcracker. All five of us kids picked the nut meats out of the cracked nuts, while my mother bustled around the kitchen making batch after batch of fudge and cookies. Mother and Daddy made a special caramel-pecan fudge that was simply wonderful, and I know that people looked forward to their Christmas packages every year, filled with divinity and fudges, stuffed dates, and sugared, decorated cookies placed around the edges for packing.

A couple of weeks before Christmas, my father went out and bought the biggest, fullest tree he could find. He usually had to cut the top off because it would be too tall for the living room ceiling. All of us would decorate it, using decorations my parents paid for dearly during the Depression, odd-looking ornaments from Germany made before the War, and very old bubble lights, along with newer balls and multicolored strings of lights. Then, under the direction of my older sister, we would carefully drape every inch of the tree with icicles until it shimmered. Packages, wrapped by aunts and cousins and our own inexpert hands, would go under the tree until the pile of gifts brushed the lower branches.

We had visitors all through the season, aunts and uncles and cousins and friends, dropping by to pick up their boxes of goodies and to leave behind presents for us. They especially came to see my grandmother, who lived with us and was the matriarch of the family. The side door was never locked. They walked in all through the day and evening, expecting that they would be welcomed and never being disappointed by my mother. My father didn't always care for the confusion, but he was often at work at night and sleeping during the day, so he missed a lot of it.

The days before Christmas were filled with anticipation, with kindness and good humor. We had all ordered up a present from Santa Claus, and knew that we would get what we wanted. No one was scolded or belittled in the days before Santa's arrival. My mother told us later, when we were adults, that when she was a child, Christmas was strictly a religious holiday, and presents were exchanged on January 6th. She preferred it that way, but that my father wanted Christmas to be a big holiday with lots of gift-giving and joy.

Santa's coming was coordinated with my father's work schedule, but of course when we were little, we didn't notice. If my father worked evenings, (3 p.m. to 11 p.m.) Santa came at night and we got our presents early in the morning on Christmas, then attended Mass. However, if he worked graveyard (11 p.m. to 7 p.m.), we might go to church first and find our presents waiting for us when we got home. We always got a "big present," something we really wanted. My parents didn't have a lot of money but they always figured out a way to make Christmas work.

When I was five, I learned to ride a bike and wanted my own bicycle for Christmas. My older sister was eleven that year and wanted a full-size bike. My father bought her a new bike, then painted her older, smaller bicycle with snazzy enamel paint and left it for me beside the tree as a present from Santa. I was thrilled and never tumbled to the fact that it wasn't new. Other than our big present, we also got several smaller presents, clothes and toys that my mother, in particular, thought we would enjoy. Since we didn't get a lot of presents during the year, except at Christmas and our birthdays, the season was really a happy time.

However, after the mess was cleared up, and the turkey dinner with all the trimmings cooked and consumed, we knew the holiday spirit would disappear and things would get back to "normal." Normal meant never knowing what was going to happen next.

The Christmas that I found out there was no Santa Claus was the occasion that I became depressed. I was seven years old and in the second grade. Mrs. Cavanaugh was my teacher, a caring woman and a dedicated teacher. Some of the boys were teasing another because he still believed in Santa Claus. He insisted that there was a Santa Claus because "He comes to my house every year." The other boys answered, "Oh, you dummy, that's just your father dressed up like Santa Claus." Then, of course, Mrs. Cavanaugh stepped in to change the subject, but my mind was going a hundred miles an hour. I kept my own counsel, but I was shaken. I had never questioned the concept of Santa Claus; he was a given at our house and here were these guys teasing another for believing in him. I was troubled all day about it. I didn't say a word at school, but I remembered that every year we left out cookies and milk for Santa, and believed completely that he brought us gifts along with every other child in the world.

When I got home that day, I asked my mother about the boys' teasing. She admitted that there was no real Santa Claus, and explained that he was but a concept of love. She explained that she and my father actually did the work of buying presents and leaving them for us. I was crushed.

Mostly I felt stupid for having believed in an elf that could travel the whole world in one night and give out presents to everyone. I should have known better, I chastised myself. I also asked my mother why she and my father had lied to me. It had been preached to me all my life that I should never lie and that lying was a terrible sin; why then, had I been lied to? For that's how I saw it, as a lie. Not as a parent would see it, as a pleasant legend that makes a child happy, but as a lie that had deceived me and made me feel small and stupid.

My mother, obviously upset by the question, just answered, "Well, it makes your father happy and he enjoys it." I crept silently away to think about the cosmic shift that had taken place in my view of the world. Not only had Christmas completely changed for me, but my mother, father, and older sister and brother had been lying to me this and other Christmas seasons because, and this floored me, simply because they enjoyed it.

Christmas was ruined for me that year, though I followed my mother's instructions and did not clue in my younger sister. I kept the secret to myself and began to keep my own counsel about my further thoughts. For, if Santa was a legend, what about God? Santa sees and hears children and knows how they behave, and so does God. Santa is made up by adults to please themselves, why not God? I had never seen God, though I had seen Santa's helpers downtown and even had my picture taken with one of them. If adults were capable of lying about one thing, why not another? If I couldn't trust my parents, how could I trust any other adults?

Though I didn't recognize it at the time, I became more and more depressed as I tried to sort out reality. I can remember sitting in a classroom during religious instruction and trying to determine why adults were all pretending to not only believe in God and but also to follow a certain moral code which they wanted so desperately to pass on to us. What was the purpose? For I knew then that they were all pretending. It was just like the Santa legend -- all made up to impress children. I finally decided that it was a power thing. It was important to them that we believe what they wanted us to believe. I can remember being really paranoid, thinking that priests and parents laughed at us behind our backs because we were so gullible.

4

Of course, I had no one I could share these thoughts with, because I thought the entire adult world was engaged in a plot against me and I, of all the children, was the only one to recognize it. I can only remember that after a few weeks, I began to feel better and that I came to the conclusion that no one could keep up such a complicated plot. The adults must really believe in what they preached. But I never really got over my feelings that the whole thing was a power play: and I never really believed in religion again.

My parents were pious and observant Catholics, and they expected the same of their children. One of the most important things to them was that we go to church daily and attend Catholic schools so we could be tutored in proper morals and in the teachings of their religion. It would have shocked and horrified my mother and father to know even part of what I was thinking, so I could not even share any of it with them. I grew up to be an atheist and don't know if my thoughts and feelings would have been different without this experience with depression when I was so young. But that's what happened and it influenced me from then on. I knew better than to discuss it with anyone. I continued to attend Mass and Catholic schools, but it was all a pretense, just as I had assumed it was for everyone else for a time.

Chapter Two: And I'm Nobody's Baby

Bipolar disorder, or manic-depressive illness, is known to be inherited. It affects between 0.5 and 1.6 percent of the total population.[2] Children of persons with bipolar disorder have an increased risk of developing the disease.   This risk is several times that of the general population; children of persons with bipolar disorder have a one in four chance of developing some kind of mood disorder, and a one in ten chance of developing bipolar disorder.[3]

---

[2] **American Psychiatric Association. (1994).** *Diagnostic and Statistical Manual of Mental Disorders.* **pp. 422-3.**

[3] **Mondimore, F.M. (1999).** *Bipolar: A Guide for Patients and Families.* **Baltimore: The Johns Hopkins Press. p. 195.**

What this means in a practical sense is that if the genes for bipolar disorder are present in your family, you are subject not only to dealing with the disease yourself, but also to be raised in a dysfunctional situation. While I can certainly see the gene at work in my nuclear family, I can also trace it back to my grandfather, whom I never met because he died years before I was born. I know him through stories I heard about him, enough to know that he suffered from it and undoubtedly passed it on to his children and grandchildren.

Here is a story I wrote about my grandmother, a strong and unique woman:

When we were teenagers we were subjected to the most boring and long-winded recitations; we would roll our eyes at each other and sigh, not believing that we had to listen, again, to what it was like for my grandmother when she was our age.

It couldn't possibly have any relevance to our lives and didn't hold any interest for us, but there we were, prisoners at the dinner table, and we had to listen again to what it was like for a sixteen-year-old bride on the prairie who had to keep house in a sod hut. She told us what it was like to have to feed her family on only black-eyed peas and sparse game because the first crop to go in after the sod was busted had to be a legume to fix nitrogen in the soil. (Hence, you must eat black-eyed peas on New Year's Day to ensure good crops in the future.) She described her struggles to keep herself, her clothes, and her kitchen clean in a house made of dirt when she had to haul water a half mile, and it was more sensible to hang the frying pan on the wash line and let the maddening and ubiquitous wind scour it than to waste water on it.

She told of the Indians who would stop in and demand that she cook for them. Sometimes it took all the food she had in the house to feed them, but she was afraid, with her husband in the fields or in town, to refuse them anything. After all, she represented those who took their lands, killed the buffalo, and left them unable to feed themselves or their children. They left her without a word, never harming her, but always in fear.

After two years of isolation, plowing, (which is a tame word for breaking the virgin sod), building a shelter, performing incredible toil in the fields,

8

hauling water, burning dried buffalo dung for fuel, starving, broiling in the sun, freezing in the winter, and living with the ever-present and infuriating wind, it did not rain, of course, when it had to and the wheat failed. With no other choice, my pregnant grandmother and her husband -- not my grandfather, for he came later, moved to Oklahoma City, where he could hope his dreams of fortune would not be so subject to the vagaries of fortune.

For he was a dreamer, with big dreams, first, of a homestead that would bring him fortune as a wheat farmer, then, in the city, with various schemes that would bring him vast wealth. Instead of wealth, he had a wife who was just a child but who could sew dresses for ladies as fine as anything they could buy back East. She became the seamstress for those who had made their fortunes.

She worked out of their home and became as much of a success as a woman could then, in the 1890s, with all of the rich ladies in town as her customers. He was known all over the city for his charm; everyone liked him and thought him a great guy. It was just too bad that he couldn't seem to find a way to support his wife and, by now, their three children. And, you know, sotto voce, he did drink too much. My grandmother, who was raised in Kentucky with all the baggage of the Southern belle -- and with all the strength of the true Southern lady -- kept her head up and her shoulder to the wheel, paid the rent, and kept up appearances. She didn't have any other choice. That is, until one day he simply pushed her too far and found the steel underneath the ladylike exterior.

He took her last $10 to town to buy groceries. When he didn't return in a reasonable amount of time, she knew he taken the money she had given him for food for the children and gone on a bender. That sweet Southern belle snapped. She knew just where to find him. She went to the Hotel Black -- the nicest hotel in Oklahoma City, where members of the territorial legislature were ensconced. She found him with three members of the legislature finishing a steak dinner, which he had bought with her hard-earned dollars. She proceeded to give those hail-fellows-well-met a piece of her mind, telling them that they knew what kind of a man he was, that they knew they were eating food bought with her money, that her children would now go hungry because of them. Furthermore, she expected them to file a bill of divorce in the territorial legislature and to get it passed for

9

her. They did. Which is how my grandmother became the first woman to get a divorce in Oklahoma territory. This was a scandal and put her even further outside respectable society than her status as a working woman had done. Afterwards, she supported her children by herself, probably much better now that she didn't have to support her husband, too.

Later she married my grandfather, who was a widower with four children. So she had seven children to care for, then finally bore my father. Still she had stories to tell of this time, of a tyrannical second husband who had a strange hatred of Catholicism. She was forced to practice her religion in secret and to baptize my father in the dead of night at a stranger's home. A husband who was so abused as a child that he was denied education and was illiterate, but so proud that no one but her was allowed to know, so she read him every word of the newspaper daily and every paper he needed to sign. A husband who periodically disappeared without warning, only to return months later, bearing diamonds as peace offerings. Meanwhile she raised eight children and kept the home fires burning, sewing to keep food on the table while he was gone. All of those children, both her own and her stepchildren alike, adored her. She later bound her daughters-in-law and sons-in-law as closely to her as her children. She died at ninety-three. There were fifty grandchildren and great-grandchildren at her funeral and a half-page obituary in the newspaper; she was one of the best-known ladies in the city.

Well, you can see how her stories just nearly bored us to tears; after all, how would these experiences have anything at all in common with what we might face in our lives? We would never make any of the mistakes she made or face any of the hardships she did or wind up alone supporting ourselves.

Proud, now, that I was given her name. Wish I'd had a tape recorder then.

This story gives little information about my grandfather, but several clues. He was illiterate because his older sisters, who raised him, refused him an education to keep him working in the fields. This doesn't seem quite right at the start. My grandmother offered many times to teach him to read and write, but he had too much pride and was too stubborn to learn. He preferred to fake it, pretending he could read, always keeping someone from the family close by to manage reading chores or he would explain that he could not sign anything without my grandmother's approval.

My grandfather was a policeman, but was well-known in the territory and later, the state for his political savvy. In the 1920s, he took a leave of absence from his job to serve as campaign manager for a gubernatorial candidate who later won. Somehow, he was not rewarded with a state position, but continued in his job as a lowly cop.

He did carry out the duties of a policeman, but also was known to hijack bootleggers and steal their shipments to sell on his own. My father knew this, but did not know what he had done the times he had to flee to Cuba to wait for things to cool down before he could return home. It was on these occasions that he brought my grandmother diamonds to ensure his welcome home. My grandmother did not approve of his departures from the straight and narrow and was displeased by his criminal activities.

He was an abusive husband and father, who beat my father and demanded that my grandmother stay away from church. She was only able to baptize my father by doing it in secret, and had to educate my father in the Catholic doctrine without his father's knowledge. My grandmother would not divorce him, as she had divorced her first husband. She felt that she had committed a terrible sin by doing so. Even though there was really no other option, her religion told her that divorce was not allowed and she went to her grave convinced that she had broken God's laws by divorcing.

I believe that through these few clues about my grandfather, it is easy to see in hindsight that he was an intelligent man who was able to carry off involvement in enterprises that took more talent than his education and background would ordinarily have prepared him for. He was stubborn and eccentric, and thought nothing of being involved in criminal activities. Perhaps it wouldn't mean as much to someone without my family history, but when the next two generations were obviously touched by bipolar disorder, it leads one to believe that the gene has long been in the family. One of my psychiatrists, at least, believed these clues significant for my diagnosis. He believed from what I told him that my grandfather clearly suffered from bipolar disorder.

In the 1950s and 60s, people believed much more in nurture than in nature. This harkened back to World War II and the theories of the Germans and Japanese, who had put so much stock in pure blood and good breeding. This was rejected in the wake of the war, and inheritance was downplayed. Especially was it not thought that mental illness was inherited. You developed mental illness from the way your parents treated you, not from your genes.

I was skeptical of this, even as a child. I could see clear behavioral patterns that seemed to depend on inheritance. For example, when I was eleven, I noted that alcoholics on one side of my family were slow, steady drinkers who might consume a fifth a day, but who were able to go to work and kept their drinking off the streets and inside their homes. (There were plenty of drinkers in my family, for they descended from my grandmothers, both of whom were Irish-Catholic. Since it was my grandmothers, we weren't raised on the politics of Ireland, but on the superstitions and religion of the island.)

Alcoholics on the other side of the family were binge-drunks; that is, they drank for a specific time, becoming horribly drunk, not making it to work and generally making fools of themselves. One, my father's double cousin*, was a wino who lived on the streets. To even my young mind, it seemed quite possible that alcoholism was inherited, and even the type genetically passed down. This observation made me more likely to look at my relatives and their behavior, and to try to relate it to possible genetic inheritance.

But, in general, in our family, people were just the way they were. There was no suspicion of mental illness. People might be a little odd, or somewhat eccentric, but that was just their personalities. I had one cousin who suffered from severe depression. She was unable to care for herself and for her children, and her mother-in-law, my aunt, let everyone know how much she considered the woman to be weak and her son to have made a mistake by marrying her. The cousin had to be hospitalized, and that just didn't happen in good families. My cousin, according to the consensus of the family, should have been able to

---

* My grandfather's brother married my grandmother's sister, so their child was my father's double cousin.

handle her problems without the help of mental health professionals.

My parents wrote her off as "stupid." If a person was mentally ill, there was no treatment except for the hospital or talk therapy. There was no percentage in being ill. You simply sucked up and did the best you could, shouldering your way through the depressions and assuming the manias were just part of life.

Who could take time off work to talk to a therapist? Wouldn't do any good, anyway. Just go to church and pray about it. Things would eventually sort themselves out.

CHAPTER THREE: I LIKE IT LIKE THAT

It was a big night at our house because my oldest sister was getting married. She was the first to leave the nest, and would be marrying in a simple church wedding the next morning. We had been planning for weeks and the big day was finally here. The house was cleaned and polished and full of guests. All four of the girls were in my big sister's bedroom, trying on pink dresses with American rose sashes, checking on hairstyles, and just generally having a giggling good time. We were all excited; this was unprecedented in our lives. Suddenly, without knocking, my father opened the door and stuck his head in. He had a last word for my sister. He didn't want to wish her well or give her a last piece of advice. He just said, "I'll be glad when you're gone. You are the one who causes all the problems around here." Then he left. Our party over, we slunk off while my sister had her cry. It was typical of my father; he was not the center of attention and the wedding had upset his life, so he took his hurt feelings out on the person he perceived to be the cause.

My mother was loving and stable. Occasionally she would become depressed, but this happened seldom. When she did become depressed, she had a tendency to see my father's side of things and you could have just flung up a chain-link fence around the house and called it a sanitarium. But most of the time we could count on our mother as a haven of sanity.

We never knew what to expect from our father. He was a brilliant man who was self-educated and knew something about everything. He could also build or repair anything. He was a great conversationalist and could explain anything to a kid. We had some wonderful dinner table conversations, but we had just as many when the tension was as thick as the beef we ate. No one said anything, then; it was too dangerous. God forbid you spill your drink; not even my grandmother could get away with that.

We never knew what would set him off. Something that was fine one day would be disastrous the next. Chaos ruled. For example, we shucked out of our shoes as soon as we came in the door in the summer. Periodically, but certainly not every time, he would get upset at the shoes lying on the floor, and then, screaming curses, would throw them all in the basement. This did not teach us to put our shoes up, but only to look for our shoes in the basement. Of course, he never asked us to simply pick up our shoes in a reasonable manner.

As another example, I can remember that I was reading the paper one day when I was about twelve. We kept our schoolbooks on a wide window ledge in the dining room when we weren't actually working on homework; that way, the books and papers were all together in the morning in the mad dash to get ready for school. We had done that since we moved into the house six years before. On this day, he suddenly asked me what all the stuff on the window ledge was. Not taking him seriously, without looking up from the paper, I answered, "Those are our books. That's where we keep them." Suddenly, he was on me. The paper was ripped from my hands, and, screaming that I would never "talk back" to him again, he was striking me. He would not hit us when mother was in the house, so obviously she was not home at that time.

When something like this happened, which was often, we kids would scatter, either going outside or upstairs, out of his sight. We stayed away until we had to assemble for a meal or until summoned by our mother. We all had our ways of staying out of the way. My older sister took dance lessons daily, becoming one of the premier dancers in the city. My brother went away to school when he was fourteen, leaving me, to my distress, without my protector. I spent most of my time in my room reading books, devouring at least one a day. My younger sister insists that she spent several years hiding in the closet.

He was unhappy that God had seen fit to give him only one boy, and let us know that he did not value girls or want them. I early expressed a desire to go to college, and he informed me that I would not, because "education is wasted on women. They just get married and have children, so there is no need for them to go to school." His children were not really people, but extensions of him. Everything we did reflected on him, so we were expected to behave impeccably, and it was a given that we would all make straight As in school. No excuses were allowed.

He had all the emotional maturity of a two-year old. He had to have his way, and he insisted on being the center of attention at all times. He had no insight, and could not see that he had problems. If anyone had problems, it was the person he was upset with at the time. He resented his children because they took my mother's time and attention away from him, and he let us know how unhappy that made him. He often told us, in so many words, that he wished we had not been born, that we kept him from doing things that he wanted to do, and periodically told us to leave the house and not come back. We would, of course, simply stay out of sight until Mother returned. We didn't tattle on him unless he got too out of control, then we would let her know that he had been hitting us. She would always calm the situation down.

Her method was to protect him from reality as much as possible and to make his life run as smoothly as possible. She handled the money because he could not be trusted to do so; she had taken over money management when they were first married during the Great Depression and it became obvious that he could not restrain his spending.

He worked at the same job for forty-three years, never receiving a promotion. He worked the night shift for the night-differential pay, but I do not believe he could have handled the social interaction with the men on the day shift. On the night shift, he worked with only one other man. I am not at all certain he would have kept his job for as long as he did without union protection. At one point in his career, he had a boss who was trying to fire him, and he reacted by becoming physically ill. Doctors could find nothing wrong with him, so he went to several clinics, some of them out-of-town prestigious hospitals. Again, no physical reason for his pain was found. Tranquilizers were prescribed. He refused to take them, and took his pain out on our mother. We would wake in the middle of the night to his cursing at her because she did not care for him and would not believe that he was sick. She finally managed it by slipping the tranquilizers into his morning juice, thus solving the problem. His pain went away. She did that for years, until he got a boss who was easier to get along with.

He seldom acted out in front of our friends, which was a blessing, but left us in the situation of hearing about what a neat father we had. We simply agreed since you couldn't explain that he was just using his company manners. However, there were times when we were dating that we wanted to sink through the floor.

He considered the parking place in front of our house to be "his." No matter that it was a public street, it was where he wanted to park his car and nobody else better park there. Our dates, in all innocence, would park their cars there. My father would come home from work and ram his car into one of our date's cars because he felt it in "his" parking place. It was difficult to explain and often ended our relationships. Those that hung in learned to park elsewhere and to tread carefully around him.

He often told us how unhappy he had been when the company he worked for intervened when he tried to enlist in the Navy, doing submarine duty, during World War II. They had insisted that his job was essential on the home front and he stayed home. All of us kids wondered how he could have possibly adjusted to military discipline and to being away from our mother. We felt that while he may have truly have been upset about missing out on the biggest happening of the century, that he was secretly relieved at not having to face the adjustment of leaving home and joining the military. For him, it would have been a tremendous wrench.

We had never heard of manic-depression or bipolar disorder, but we knew our father had problems. We didn't know the diagnosis, or even that what he had was considered a mental illness. My mother handled it in such a matter-of-fact way that all of us simply lived our lives around how my father was; we just adjusted our lives to fit his.

Later, when I got married, I paid for my own simple wedding. I let my mother buy me a new dress because she begged me to. But I did not have my father walk me down the aisle or have any part in the planning or execution of the wedding because I never forgot those words he said to my sister. I wasn't going to give him an opportunity to rain on my parade.

If he was depressed, he was stressed out, and in the extreme, expressed it with somatic disorders. He refused to accept the fact that his depression could cause him to be ill, but my mother handled it. When he became manic, he could be pleasant and even fun for a while, but eventually he would become irritable and finally out of control. Everything, even normal problems of living, was too much for him to manage. My mother took most problems off his back and tried to make his life run as smoothly as possible. What she did not know is that she could not smooth out his moods no matter how hard she tried. Chaos would always be the rule of the day, depression swapping with mania, both of them demanding more of him than he could handle.

After my mother's death, he fell into a deep depression, and was prescribed antidepressants. It was the first time he was offered medication for any of his moods. Of course, he refused to take them. He proved that he could not live without my mother by dying of "respiratory failure" exactly 51 weeks after her death. No one but family came to his funeral, and not even his children were saddened by his death -- only by the fact that he had lived such an unhappy life.

Chapter 4: But Then Again...Maybe

I've always been told I was stubborn and single-minded, even as a small child. My parents told me that as soon as I could speak, I demanded a cat. As soon as I could toddle, I brought home the neighbor's cats and every stray cat I ran across. I made it clear I wanted a white cat with blue eyes, and on Easter after my second birthday, my aunt, who lived on a farm, found a white kitten with blue eyes in her neighborhood . The kitten was placed in my Easter basket. Finding the kitten curled up in my Easter basket is my earliest memory. Snowball was my cat until I was 22, and I've had cats in my life ever since.

I was born in 1945, shortly before the end of World War II. My parents had two children before the war, and had decided not to have any until after the end of the war and the world was more settled. However, D-Day was such a victory and such a precursor to the war's end, that they celebrated it by getting pregnant, and I was the result. My growing-up years were in the '50s, which most people today look back on nostalgically. I believe they have forgotten McCarthyism and the Korean War. The 1950s had its problems, too.

It was when I was three, watching the newsreels in the movies, that I developed the great fear of my life. It grew to be an almost irrational fear that has haunted me all of my life, hatched by watching the refugees, both Indian and Muslim, forced from their homes by the partition of India in 1948. I can remember asking my mother, "Why don't they go home?" and her terrifying answer, "They don't have homes anymore." From then on, scenes of refugees, fleeing wars, unrest and natural disasters awakened a deep fear in me that someday I would be left homeless, with only the belongings I could carry.

I was always fascinated by the written word, and I spent a great deal of my time trying to find someone who would read to me. Since I could listen to books by the hour, it was a chore for everyone, but somehow I talked them into it. Resources were my mother, my father, and my older brother and sister. There was no television at that time, (we didn't get one until I was seven) so reading was a prime entertainment. At Christmas, my father always read "A Christmas Carol," out loud to us, taking on the dialect and the differing voices of the characters, and we loved it.

I got into the "I want to do it myself" stage early. I "went for a walk" at the age of two, throwing everyone into a panic. However, a "nice man" brought me home, knowing that a child that age shouldn't be walking around alone. I didn't understand why everyone was so upset. I can remember demanding to dress myself and my mother allowing me to do so. However, I didn't quite pull it off as I hadn't yet been introduced to the idea of shoes going on to the right feet. Everyone laughed at me when I clomped out, triumphantly dressed, with my shoes on the wrong feet. I was humiliated. I thought I had done so well and to find out that I had messed up. I had been laughed at and that was too much. The next day, determined not to make any more mistakes, I carefully brought out my socks and asked which feet they went on, only to be greeted by peals of laughter. Humiliation again. I wonder why parents forget that children are like cats -- they don't like to be laughed at.

The "I want to do it myself" also applied to reading. I got as tired of trying to finagle reading out of others as they got tired of reading to me. I wanted to do it myself. Somehow, it had been conveyed to my mother that only "experts" could teach children to read; that parents would botch it up for the experts if they tried to teach a child anything before the school could get to them. So she forbade my siblings to teach me anything, though they were willing if it would get me off their backs, and she just told me that I would have to wait for first grade. She promised me that I would learn to read in first grade. That quieted me for a while.

In kindergarten, I learned how to tie shoes, which hadn't been an issue before since I seldom wore anything but slip-ons or sandals, how to tell time, the compass directions, the basic nature of men, and that people are not to be trusted. Heavy lessons for a five-year old.

The school was only two blocks away, so I was allowed to walk home. Imagine my terror when a boy starting chasing me home! I had never run into aggressive behavior before; there were many children on my block and we all played happily together. After I arrived home in a state a couple of times, my father told me not to run, but to stand my ground and punch him the next time he tried to chase me. I did so, and suddenly I had a boyfriend who walked me home every day and paid attention to me at school. The shock came when I entered first grade and my "boyfriend" no longer acknowledged me. He was too grown up for me then.

The harder lesson was when, after six weeks of school, our kindly, middle-aged teacher brought in a young teacher, Ms. Sauber, and said that she was taking over the class. Ms. Sauber, the next Monday, said that the older teacher was on vacation and would be back later. Well, I kept asking when the original teacher, whom I had really liked, would be back and kept being put off. Finally, I told my mother I didn't understand the situation. My mother told me that she was upset that I had been told that the first teacher would be back, because she had cancer and would not be returning. I never trusted Ms. Sauber again and wondered why she felt she had to lie to me. I had waited for weeks for a teacher to come back who never would.

But finally, after surviving a not very challenging year of kindergarten in 1951, I was going to start real school and I was going to learn to read! I don't think I was ever ready for anything like I was for that. I was so eager to start school, I was not the slightest bit ambivalent about it. I was not at all frightened about leaving home to go to school all day; all I wanted was to learn to read. My brother dropped me off in the first-grade classroom and I was set.

All of us kids attended a small Catholic school about a mile and a half from our home. It was staffed primarily by nuns and had, compared to public schools, fairly small class sizes. We had a regular curriculum except that we also had religion classes, taught by the priests who lived in the rectory and said Mass at that the Cathedral the school was attached to. There was no scandal attached to these priests -- they were caring human beings who would never have thought of hurting any of us. My brother was a server at Mass and we all attended daily.

But I didn't learn to read. I can remember weeping after the first week because I hadn't learned anything. My parents counseled patience and promised I would learn. It seemed like forever, but I think I got my reader, "Dick and Jane," after the first nine weeks. And how disappointing that was. I was crushed. To think that I was going to read something that short, with so few words, that boring, for nine weeks. My mother couldn't stand it any longer. She said that if I could master the reader, which I did in a day, she would help me with words in anything I wanted to read. And I started reading. I knew if I asked her a word, I'd better remember it, because she was too busy to ask her over and over. Besides, I wanted to show everyone that I could do it. I would spell a word out loud and whoever was around would tell me what it was. Slowly I gained a vocabulary, and when no one was around I'd figure out the word by context. By golly, I was learning to read -- finally.

I was reading a Nancy Drew book by the weekend. And there was no turning back after that. My mother just asked me to not let them know at school that I was so far ahead and we continued to read clandestinely, with her taking me to the library on the weekends. I read all of the children's standards and graduated to adult books while I was still working on "readers" at school. Of course, my reading got me in trouble, eventually, because I wasn't able to keep it secret. I checked a book out of the school library because I liked the title, "The White Rose." But when I got into the book, it had words I couldn't figure out, like "Gestapo." I also couldn't understand the situations the characters were involved in; I just didn't have the experience to relate to them. I didn't want to admit that I couldn't read it, so just quietly returned the book. When I checked it back in, a nun saw what I had been reading and went ballistic. The book was obviously too old for me and I shouldn't have been exposed to it. My parents were called in for a conference. My father questioned me about the book before the conference, and I admitted that I hadn't been able to understand it, so hadn't read it. I was completely confused about why I was in trouble.

My father went to the conference loaded for bear. The nuns were all bent out of shape out by my reading such a book, which I found out later, was about the underground movement at the University of Munich during World War II. (I've never been able to find a copy of the book since, but I would love to read it and find out what all the fuss was about.) He, who had also had his reading questioned when he was a child, explained quite simply that "a book that a child can understand is not too old for her; if it is too old for her, then she won't be able to understand it. No problem." Then he pointed out that I had gained access to the book at the school library, not at home. So, thanks to me, many books in the library were locked up and denied to younger students; I always felt faintly that I had done something wrong; but the support I received at home for my eclectic reading was never withdrawn.

One major happening that I remember was being approached by a teenage boy on the walk home one day when I was seven, in the second grade. It was odd enough being approached by a teen-age boy; then he said, "I'll give you a quarter to go into the cemetery with me." We were walking past a cemetery that stretched for about half a mile. I knew that teenage boys should not be interested in seven-year old girls, I also knew that strangers did not give money to little girls for nothing. I asked him "Why?" and he just said that he wanted to show me something. I said, "No, my big brother usually walks me home and he will be by on his bicycle any minute." To emphasize that, I kept turning around and checking behind me every few steps. My brother was a safety officer who helped the little ones across the street after school and he did usually catch up with me and walk the rest of the way with me. On this day, he was nowhere to be seen, of course. The guy kept upping the ante, finally offering me five dollars. I wouldn't bite. I just felt the situation wasn't right, even though I had no idea what he wanted. Finally, just before he shoved off, he stopped in the middle of the street, turned and hollered back that he had wanted to "fuck me." I was confused by all this and didn't work up the nerve to tell my mother about it for several years. When I did tell her, my instincts were right; she was upset. But we didn't have to walk home from school so often after that.

My sisters, brother and I were expected to behave well, so we did. We were expected to make straight As, so we did. My major memory of the school is one of boredom. Sometimes I read books during class, keeping an ear open for what was happening. When the nuns found out they couldn't catch me not paying attention, they left me alone. I soaked up everything they taught me and learned more from my father at home, who was able to supplement my lessons. I was clueless in arithmetic and math and stayed that way for the rest of my life. No one could ever explain it so that I understood it. Ever.

However, in the fifth grade, I had a lay teacher, Ms. Jarboe, who felt that I needed extra attention and extra work. For example, when the class studied the Civil War in history, she had me read "Uncle Tom's Cabin" and give a report on it. And so on. She will never know how grateful I was for this; it relieved the boredom and made me feel special.

When I was ten, my brother, who was fourteen, went away to a seminary prep school for boys preparing who would eventually study for the priesthood. It was the first time I saw my mother cry except at the death of a relative. I was left without my closest friend in the family, and the one who I felt was my protector. He knew how to stay out of trouble and often kept me out of it, too. We had spent many hours together, even sneaking off to the semi-pro baseball games when we weren't supposed to leave the neighborhood. When we did things like that, I was his partner in crime. He had always let me tag along, even though I was four years younger and female to boot.

I don't remember being bothered by my illness, except when I found out about Santa Claus. There were ups and downs in my life, but I handled everything by retreating into books. I read just about anything, from the "Black Stallion" to Dickens. I could read a book a day with no problem, after I finished my homework. This left little time for interaction with family members, and made my mother nervous. She tried to limit my reading, but that was like limiting a waterfall. It just couldn't be done.

I remember when I was about ten my mother interrupted my reading for something, and I objected. She said, "Well, when you have children, you will never have time to read a book again." (Not a good way to influence me to have children.) I had already decided that I did not want to live my life like my mother, dependent on a man with a houseful of kids to care for. I answered, "I'm not going to have children." She was genuinely startled. She said, "Oh, but you have to have children." I said, "No, I don't." I knew nothing about birth control, but I instinctively knew my life would be different.

I had close girlfriends in my sixth, seventh, and eighth grades, Pat and Maria. We did little but experiment with make-up, watch "American Bandstand" and listen to DJ's on the radio, but it did bring me out of myself a bit. Maria had a huge crush on Elvis, but I couldn't understand being in love with someone you never met. I couldn't join her in that. I liked Buddy Holly for his music and was crushed by his early death, and kept up with most of the popular singers. Boyfriends were not for me at that age. Most of the guys were gangly and not interested in girls then, anyway. I graduated from eighth grade in a beautiful pink sheath with a jacket my grandmother made for me. My parents were not there, since they went to my brother's high school graduation in San Antonio.

CHAPTER 5: I'M NOBODY'S VALENTINE

Starting high school wasn't like starting first grade. I didn't go into it with the same high spirits and confidence. The thirty or so students I had gone to school with for eight years would be joined by classes from all the other Catholic schools from the north side of town; so I would be in a much larger class made up mostly of strangers. My best friend, Maria, was going to public school, so I was feeling somewhat alone when I entered school in a class that was made up of about 120 freshmen. And I didn't do well.

I know now that I was in the first manic phase that I can remember. Many bipolar people will state that their manic phase is wonderful, soaring, and filled with creativity. Mine is not. I feel good and it certainly is better than being depressed, but it is not really positive. Oh, I feel confident and feel that I could take on the world, but the effect it has on others is not lost on me. When I was fourteen, surrounded by people I wanted to be popular with, and striking out, it was confusing and the fact that I couldn't control made it unbearable. When I'm manic, I feel like someone is playing pool in my brain. My thoughts carom off each other, bouncing off each other. I can't think in a straight line and nothing makes much sense. My manic phase is marked by constant talking, characterized by jumping from subject to subject. This is known as "pressured speech" and has the effect on others that you are trying to dominate all conversations, often about things that others are not at all interested in. Not a way to gain popularity. And yet, even conscious of it, I am powerless to turn it off. It just keeps flowing, with me having no control over it. I wanted to make friends with these new boys and girls -- especially the girls, as I wasn't yet too interested in the boys, but I sabotaged myself. Mania is also characterized by in an inability to concentrate, which makes paying attention in school, doing homework, and grasping concepts difficult. While I worked just as hard as ever in school, my grades slipped some and I brought home some Bs. Poor judgment is also a hallmark, which is also not a way to become popular. Making stupid remarks, doing stupid things will turn people off rapidly. I also had a tendency to lose my temper over tiny things and to be irritable.

I saw myself pushing people away and not being able to control myself. I couldn't figure out what was wrong, and could not change my behavior. I asked my mother to allow me to sleep downstairs, in the room that had been my brother's because I couldn't sleep and they would have been after me to stop reading or to turn off my light at a reasonable time. But I simply couldn't sleep; sleep didn't come just because I turned off the light. Sleeplessness is a characteristic of both mania and depression; I have fought to sleep all my life. I wish I could tell you how many doctors I went to that I told "I don't sleep." Not one of them, until I finally found a sympathetic psychiatrist in my thirties, ever really believed that I simply did not sleep. I moved downstairs to where my parents could not monitor me. I read until Jack Paar came on at 10:30, then watched him until he went off air at 12:30, perhaps reading some more before I finally fell asleep. I had to get up at 6:30, but didn't seem to be tired and got through my school day just fine. It didn't strike me as odd that I was operating on so little sleep; I just felt that I didn't need much.

Of course, after a while I slid off the manic phase and went into a more normal phase before plunging into depression. This became so usual to me that I assumed it was normal and never suspected that I was in any way ill or unusual. After all, this had been modeled for me all my life at home. My freshman year was not a happy one, but I was going to a good school that challenged me intellectually and I was happy about that. I just felt like a square peg in a round hole, but I was able to make a good friend, Jo Jean, who was not Catholic but was attending the school because her parents wanted the discipline and superior academics for her.

As I came down, I slowly adjusted to my new school and liked some aspects of it. The teachers were, for the most part, good and I enjoyed the social sciences and English courses especially. I finally made it through the year but did not feel good about it. Depression, of course, was not pleasant. It was accompanied also be sleeplessness, lack of concentration and the rather more upsetting thoughts of suicide. I often thought of killing myself; at that age I didn't think of methods but simply of dying to make the pain of my life stop. However, at that age, I also had the hope of getting out of the home situation and ordering my own life as an adult. Somehow, I thought that would be better.

Every summer all my life my father loaded all of us up and we took a National Lampoon-type summer vacation. They were just awful -- seven people in an un-air-conditioned car in August with the goal of seeing how many miles could be driven in two weeks. I knew every greasy spoon on Route 66 and can especially remember the time spent by the side of the road with my father changing tires. All of us in the same motel rooms at night for two weeks -- way too much intimacy. While the trips were nightmares, they're the kind of thing that I'm glad I did a half-century later -- I learned a lot and saw of lot of things I wouldn't have otherwise. Still, I wouldn't do it again for anything. The trips were taken in furtherance of my father's hobby -- model railroading. We saw trains and stations ad nauseam.

There was one really good part to every vacation -- the first three days. The first three days every year were spent driving to the Gulf Coast to spend time in Galveston. No matter where we were going on vacation -- California, Wyoming, Utah, Colorado, South Dakota, we always went to Galveston first. When we were little, we didn't question that part of the trip -- it was just a great time on the beach before the long, hot days cooped up in the car.

Later, we realized that little side trip resulted from a promise my father made when he and my mother became engaged at the University of Texas. She was born and raised in Houston and her biggest reservation about moving to Oklahoma City was leaving her beloved Gulf behind. My father promised her she could visit it once a year, and, to his credit, kept his promise for forty years. We loved our trips to the beach as much as our mother -- Galveston with its white beaches, palm trees, and colorful houses seemed exotic after central Oklahoma. I can still smell the ocean and remember the sunburns we invariably got running around on the beach collecting seashells and playing in the surf. We visited relatives in Texas and just generally had a good time. Texas and Oklahoma were our stomping grounds growing up -- we traveled all over the region.

That summer between my freshman and sophomore year in high school, something else happened that was extremely important to me. I won a radio contest whose prize was a "date" with the Four Preps. The Four Preps were a popular pop/folk quartet. Their "26 Miles" stayed on the charts for 26 weeks in 1957, and they followed up with another huge hit, "Big Man," in 1958. Their later hits, "Down By the Station," "Cinderella" and "Got a Girl" combined their irreverent humor with a infectious beat and their unique harmony kept them on top.

As the winner, I would have dinner and enjoy special time backstage with the Preps. I would then have a front row seat for their concert. I was enormously excited, but also cautious and more than a little skeptical. I figured that, of course, the Preps were being paid to have this "date" with me, and I was pretty sure that they, being big stars and all, would not be too interested in a 14-year old fan. They had just come from singing in "Gidget," one of the most successful teenage movies of all time. They were huge; I had visions of being ignored all evening. But, I'd get to see a concert, so it wouldn't be a total loss. That's what I kept telling myself, so I wouldn't be disappointed.

My best friend, Jo Jean, helped me pick out my outfit and I nervously met the Preps for dinner. I was surprised to find out that they were funny and seemed to be interested in my life; they made me feel welcome. Marv, the high tenor, was particularly kind to me and made me feel special. The others were Glen, the baritone, Bruce, the lead singer, and Ed, the bass.

Then it was on to the concert. Anyone who ever saw a Preps performance, remembers that they didn't just sing their harmony hits - they put on a whole show, with Ed, Glen, and especially long-suffering Marv, playing straight men to Bruce's incessant clowning.

I felt so close to them that every year after that I'd find out when they'd be in town and make arrangements to go backstage. And each year they welcomed me. Now I had someone to have a crush on -- I had developed a full teenage crush on Marv. And my father, to his disgust, had to schedule his vacation around the Preps' gig every summer.

Chapter 6: And I'm Nobody's Pearl

I was a little more comfortable returning to school my sophomore year. My sister would be coming to high school every day with me, and I was a bit more sure of myself. However, Jo Jean was transferring to public school, so I would be, again, without my closest friend in school. Jo Jean and I did stay friends all through high school and she was a loyal friend through all the pangs of adolescence. I did well in my classes and enjoyed most of them, except math, but there was one that was a huge exception. My English teacher, who was new to the school that year, took one look at me, in class, and in front of everyone, announced, "I don't like your looks."

This was devastating. My permanent teeth had grown in crooked when I was about nine and I was, of course, extremely self-conscious about how I looked. Before I could get braces, which I desperately needed and which I was very much looking forward to, I had to have extensive oral surgery and preparation. I was in the midst of that during a time when teenagers are conscious of their looks and what people think of them. I couldn't seem to please this person after that. She said that I didn't sit respectfully in my seat, and accused me of reading trash when she saw that I had a paperback book (it was a text for another class). I did my usual level of work but was unhappy in her class and I am sure it showed. When I received a "C" midterm my mother broke her rule about never interfering with our school life and went to see the principal. She couldn't fathom one of her children getting a "C" in English, and she especially could not understand it coming from me. I never heard what happened in that conference or what was said, but I suddenly started getting "A"s again and stopped having problems with that teacher.

I did "bloom" early and had, I must say, quite a figure for a fifteen-year old. I was rather surprised when a classmate called one night. I had never really spoken to this boy. He was in a couple of classes and I knew who he was. He asked me, with no preamble, "How much do you charge?" I hung up the phone and cried. I had never acted in a way to bring this on. I had never even had a date. I couldn't possibly see how I could have a "reputation" without having done anything to get one. It was all quite upsetting and made me even less likely to date in my school. I avoided him for the next three years and we never spoke again. As an adult, I assume that he was dared by some others to do it, but as a kid, it devastated me.

I read about bullies in school today and am surprised and mystified. Even though my looks made me a real target for kids, no one ever made fun of me to my face except for that one instance and those were the only problems I had with a student and teacher. I was respected for my brains, even though I was not popular and certainly not part of the "in" crowd. My school was top-drawer academically; when we graduated, 103 of the 105 seniors went straight to college. We were encouraged to think and had quite a bit of freedom of thought and speech, considering that it was a Catholic school.

On my sixteenth birthday I was finally scheduled to get my braces. Everyone felt sorry for me that I had to get them on my birthday, but I was so happy to get them I didn't care. In fact, I considered them a great birthday present. While the dentist was working in my mouth, my mother mentioned to him that I was sixteen that day. He said, "Let me see -- what was I doing sixteen years ago today? " He recounted that he was on Iwo Jima, treating trench foot cases because he was the only one around with healthcare training. He and my mother went into a discussion of the war, and sitting there silently, it made me realize just how recent World War II had been, though it hadn't been part of my experience.

I had always been fascinated by the War because when I was small, it seemed that every other sentence began, "Now, when the war was on, .." or, "During the war,.." I was able to patch together vignettes of the war, and slowly learned that Hitler in Germany was the bad guy and that the Japanese had attacked us at Pearl Harbor. (In fact, I had gone through a short period, when I found out that Hitler's fate was not known at the time, of being afraid of strangers until I was assured that Hitler was not to be discovered in Oklahoma City.)

The thing that mystified me was why then, if the problems were with Germany and Japan, why did we promptly attack North Africa? So I started reading about the war at a young age and knew more about it than most people my age as a teenager. I did not have to be taught about the Holocaust, because I had learned about it on my own. And I had managed to solve the North Africa attack mystery by reading. When I was small, I felt like it would be stupid to ask questions about that -- everyone else seemed to understand it, and I felt dumb for not knowing the answers. I often felt that way, being raised in a family that seemed to know so much, so I tried to find out answers for myself so I could join in discussions without feeling left behind.   World War II was more important in my life than I realized at the time. My parents had decided to have a child when the war was over; when D-day was announced, they celebrated what they knew was the beginning of the end and I was born nine months later. I didn't figure that out until I was sixteen years old. At my birthday party fifty years later, I wore a T-shirt celebrating the fifty-year anniversary of D-day.

Chapter 7: When You Get Right Down To It

When my mother was pregnant with my baby sister, her fifth child, we lived in a tiny four bedroom, one-bath home. She had never liked the house, and now threatened to move out herself if we didn't find a roomier home. There were my father and her, my grandmother (my father's mother), my oldest sister, my brother, me, and my younger sister. They looked in the older part of town, closer to downtown and found two-story prairie homes that were owned by older couples. The houses had been allowed to run down.

My father found one that he thought he could fix up. It was huge, with a big living and dining room and kitchen along with a small bedroom and bath, on the first floor, and four large bedrooms and two small bedrooms upstairs with a full bath. There was a basement for his hobbies and workbench. We moved between my first and second years in school. My parents loved it, but my little sister and I hated it. There was a lot more room, but no children in the neighborhood. It was all older people and we were used to lots of kids to play with. It took some adjustment, but we learned to love the old house. Within twenty years the neighborhood had become a "historic district" and many more young people had moved in. My father worked on the house for thirty years and made a nice profit when he sold it in 1985.

We were also pretty far away from school, which left us out of many school activities, especially spontaneous get-togethers. I did not get my driver's license when I turned sixteen because my father was so picky with his cars; I didn't want to be responsible for any dings or scratches. However, by the start of my junior year in school, my mother insisted that I get it so I could take some of the driving off her back. In September, I got my license and started making the commute with my sister to high school. I used my father's car if he was working nights, my mother's if he was on the day shift.

This also meant that Jo Jean and I or my sister and I had wheels if we wanted to go somewhere. We were allowed to use my father's car if he were at work; we just had to return to his job, drop of his car, and walk the few blocks to our house . My mother was also happy to let us use her car if we ran her errands for her. My father's car was a little green 1953 Chevy; I just loved it. It's major flaw was that it would not stay in first gear for more than fifteen feet, so you had to learn to shift rapidly into second. Many a young man was impressed by my ability to speed-shift later in life. At one point the car was stolen but found less than a block away; obviously, the thief was thrown by being suddenly left in neutral in the middle of an intersection.

The best times in high school were when my father worked the four to midnight shift. He worked three weeks on and one off. For three weeks, it was just my mother, grandmother, and us kids at home in the evenings. We had casual meals and everything was low-key. We saw little, if anything, of my father and everything went along on an even keel until he was off for that one week. Then it was back to dealing with formal evening meals that were usually tense, trying not to set him off, and staying out of his way.

One of our neighbors was a sweet lady who made extra money by renting out rooms in her house. The FAA facility was in Oklahoma City and men came for short periods -- usually six or eight weeks -- to train. Some of these men would rent rooms in Mrs. Barlow's house and we made friends with them. They were usually family men who enjoyed sitting on the porch with us in the evenings after class and occasionally taking us somewhere for ice cream. On Sunday mornings, they would join us for one of my mother's legendary biscuit and gravy breakfasts. People treasured these invitations and we often had as many as twenty people for breakfast. The biscuit recipe was my grandmother's true southern biscuits with cream gravy, ham, and Canadian bacon served with eggs and fruit.

The fall of my junior year, an interesting single man moved into Mrs. Barlow's. He was tall, blond and blue-eyed. We made sure to get an introduction and discovered that he was an ex-FBI fingerprint clerk from Texas who was now training with the FAA. And he was single. We folded him into the family immediately, and he was happy to join us for meals and to take the girls out for fun. He paid special attention to me. Eddie was in his twenties and I thought I had died and gone to heaven. I'd never so much as had a date and suddenly this good-looking older guy was paying attention to me. We never had any real dates, but I was hoping. However, after about a month, he told me that he had gotten back together with his girlfriend and that they were to be married. But, he had a brother who was a freshman at the University of Oklahoma in Norman (about thirty miles away) and he would like to fix me up with Jim.

I was horribly disappointed by the denouement of my non-relationship and not planning on being too pleased with this blind date. But it would be first real date, and was certainly better than nothing.

Jim called me for the date and showed up in a clone of my father's car. He was huge, 6 feet 2 inches by 220 pounds and turned out to be on the freshman football team. Oklahoma University football ran through my blood. My uncle was a star football player at OU, and having been raised only thirty miles from the university during their glory years, I was quite naturally a fan. So this didn't hurt. He had an unfashionable crew-cut, glasses, but was good-looking with grey-green eyes, and, unlike his brother, quite shy. Having been friends with his brother, I felt comfortable with him right away. He was polite and this first date, for dinner and a movie, was great. We both enjoyed the movie and he promised to call again.

He did call, and invited me to a dance at OU for the freshman football team. We had a good time, and he didn't seem to be embarrassed by my youth or by my braces. I liked him more each time I saw him, as I broke through his reserve and discovered the good person beneath his shyness. He took me to breakfast with the team and showed me the football dorm, and my parents started attending freshman games with me. He even gave me his high school letter jacket, which reached almost to my knees. But I was proud to wear it and to feel, for the first time, that I really had a boyfriend. Once he even took me to a recruiting party for new players; I felt that I really belonged and that he must really care for me.

There was no sex involved; just the usual groping and necking, sometimes difficult because, if we were at home, Snowball, my cat, insisted on sitting between us. Snowball wanted Jim to know that I was valuable to him and that I belonged to him. At this time, birth control pills had just been introduced and were impossible for a minor to obtain. I had no moral objections to sex before marriage, but a pregnancy meant that I would have to drop out of school and more than anything, I was determined to go to college. Also, women who had premarital sex were considered to not be the kind that a man would marry -- they got a "reputation," which was just about the worse thing that could happen to a "nice" girl. A nice guy would never ask such a girl for sex, either. It was all very frustrating. Add to all this that abortion was illegal and difficult and expensive to obtain and you have a whole generation of people who just didn't have sex, or, if they did, paid for it dearly. After watching my mother and her marriage for all these years, also, I had decided that I never wanted to be dependent on a man for my livelihood.

For Christmas I gave Jim a key chain with a silver OU symbol and a little football; he gave me a rhinestone pendant. I treasured it and wore it every day. I had fallen in love with him and hoped to have a future with him. However, I was still only seventeen and was caught completely off-guard when we were embracing in my front yard one night and he said, "I want to get married." Instead of explaining that college was so important to me and that I was afraid that if I got married before I went to school, I would end up supporting my husband's schooling as had happened to so many of my friends, that I just said, "But I have to go to college." He said, "You can go to college, I'll send you." I didn't believe it, and the subject was dropped. So often women who married men who were in college ended up working while he went to college. I didn't want that to happen. I just sort of assumed that there would be plenty of time to talk about it in the future.

Unfortunately, I went into another manic phase, and when he told me that he couldn't take me to my junior prom because he had to study, I said, "Well, if you won't take me, then you don't need to come back at all!" He took me seriously, and nothing I said or did would bring him back. I spent the next several years wondering how differently my life would have turned out if I had not run him off. He was such a calm, resolute person of such high character that I had a fantasy that we could have made it even with my illness. That's something that I will never know, but I regret destroying that relationship almost more that anything else I've done in my life.

The fact that he got married the next year and that I watched him play football for the next three did not help. Every time I picked up the newspaper or heard about the team, I was reminded of what a stupid mistake I had made. Even when I was four hundred miles away in college, I heard he made the All-American team and he was on national television. I kicked myself for years over Jim.

CHAPTER 8: WHAT I SEEM TO FIND

Summers found me in Houston with my older sister and her husband, away from my parents, and dating grown-up airmen from Ellington Air Force Base. I started my senior year in school in 1962 not thinking I was ending something, but that I was preparing to start college. During my junior year, the principal of the school had called my parents in to tell them I had scored in the top two percent of the population in IQ. He wanted to encourage them to send me to college. I wanted to go to the University of Oklahoma, only a few miles down the road, but my parents made it clear I had to attend a Catholic college, preferably a girl's school. There were no Catholic colleges in Oklahoma, and I couldn't travel far because of finances, so I applied to a few in Texas and Kansas.

I later overheard my father say that if I didn't go to a Catholic school I would "get pregnant." I had no intention of getting pregnant, as that would end my education, but there was no arguing with him, so I didn't try. I also had to win a scholarship, because there wasn't enough money to pay for a private school. My father thought the worst thing that could happen to him was that one of his daughters would get pregnant out of wedlock. He never thought past the scandal to what it would mean to us or to a child; he was just thinking of what people would think of him if such a thing would happen. It would make him look bad. "What would the neighbors think?" was one of his refrains.

I remember the Cuban Missile Crisis that fall and how frightening it was. It was all we could discuss in class and out of it and suddenly all the boys felt grown-up as they talked about how it could affect their futures. It was weeks of fear and a few days of pure terror. We felt President Kennedy had done the right thing when he defused the crisis and got everything back on track.

My mother had no ambitions for her girls except that they be house-wives and perhaps teachers, but she thought college was an excellent place to meet men who would make good husbands. My father basically thought college was a waste for women. I had long rejected the role of the housewife, and when I was small, I had learned that women were allowed to work during World War II and had secretly hoped for a war so I, too, would be allowed to work. Certainly, the roles of working women were limited. Very few jobs were open to women, mostly those of teacher and nurse, and I had decided to be a history teacher, because I enjoyed the study of history and had come to the conclusion that I could do a much better job than the coaches that were foisted off on me in high school history classes. I had every intention of obtaining a degree, but my parents thought I would drop out after a year or two to get married. That is what my older sister had done, with their full approval. I didn't know it at the time, but they had no intention of helping me through four years of college.

I did not want to have children. My mother couldn't begin to understand that, and actually, didn't believe it, so I couldn't discuss my feelings with her. I didn't know why, but I had no maternal feelings. I did not think babies were cute. But I was rather afraid of them and the responsibility they represented. I was afraid that I would treat my children as my father had treated us, as an inconvenience. I thought perhaps my feelings would change, because I did assume that I would eventually get married. After all, everyone did.

I had also watched my oldest sister have four babies in five years. Each time she suffered from post-partum depression, and all the comfort the priest could give her was to tell her to have more babies so she wouldn't have time to be concerned with herself. I saw her getting more and more depressed and less functional, her life shrinking into itself and I didn't want that for myself.

My vocational ambitions were even more limited, more than I even knew, because I couldn't type worth a green bean. I had taken classes in typing, but simply didn't have the hand-eye coordination necessary to be a good typist. It frustrated me to no end, because I tried so hard, and my sister could type 100 words per minute. I made "Cs" in typing. This upset my parents, who assumed that I simply wasn't trying.

Luckily, my typing grades did not count much toward getting a scholarship, but they did knock my rank in the class down to sixth.

Both my sister and I were in the National Honor Society, but I was considered the rowdy one, first for wearing Jim's letter jacket to school, which was against the rules (no, I don't know why) and then, in my senior year, for dating a college student who came from way across town -- the wrong side of town. It was almost a scandal. I couldn't understand, because I had been around for four years, and none of the guys I was in school with had ever asked me out. So what was the big deal?

Also, my friend Jo Jean was getting married and wanted me in her wedding party. She was being married in a Baptist church, since she was Baptist. I was told the Catholic Church would not allow a member to take part in a Protestant wedding. I absolutely refused to understand that and was upset. I still don't understand the reasoning. My parents took my upset as another sign of rebelliousness -- after all, after the priest explained that I couldn't take part in the wedding, I should have calmly taken his word for it, instead of insisting that it was a stupid ruling.

On my eighteenth birthday I was home from school because I was sick when I received a letter from Mount St. Scholastica College in northeastern Kansas. They offered me a "Honors at Entrance" full tuition scholarship. It was a girl's Catholic school in a small town; exactly what my parents wanted for me. They were thrilled. I was less happy, but at least had a school that I could go to. There was a boy's school in the same town; it seemed like a waste of facilities to me. (The schools have merged now.) At that time, I did not know that a minor could go to court and become emancipated; and I am not certain that a court would have gone along with it at the time. I was still a minor and had little choice about my life.

That was driven home a few weeks later when I received a letter from the University of Oklahoma offering me a full scholarship that would pay room, board, books, and tuition and would give me entrance into a special honors program that would allow me to receive a BA in three years. I wanted it more than anything, but my parents wouldn't hear of it. I had my scholarship to a Catholic girl's school, and even though they would have to pay my room and board, they were determined I would attend the college of their choice. I -- I had no choice in the matter. I never, the rest of my life, got over the disappointment of having to turn down the scholarship and the honors program at OU. I didn't even know at the time what an opportunity I was rejecting, but I realized it later and felt even worse. I have regretted it ever since.

When we graduated, 103 of the 105 students in my class were going on to college. I had attended an extraordinary high school, though I did not realize it at the time, that had prepared me well for college. Oklahoma's youngest governor, "Ed" Edmondson, spoke at our graduation and we finished up with the summer to prepare for college.

Chapter 9: Is Some Girl Singing

We drove into the small town of Atchison, Kansas in the fall. The country around it was strange to me, with hills and the Missouri River only five blocks away. I'd never been around a large river before, and this one was huge. It actually had boats and barges on it. I'd never seen river traffic before. In the winter, it froze solid. The town was also old, and this also was strange to me. Oklahomans consider any building older than themselves to be old.

I always felt like I missed something, because that was the weekend that Martin Luther King gave his "I Have a Dream" speech and I was oblivious to it. My newspaper reading was interrupted, and I had no access to television. I don't know how long it was before I even heard of the speech.

It was my first look at the college and I liked what I saw. It was an old school, founded after the Civil War, but with new dorms and a nice student union building.   There was a nip in the air in the evenings, which was odd for the end of August.   There were only about four of us from south of Kansas, most of the students came from Iowa, Kansas, Missouri, and Nebraska.   They thought our accents hilarious and wouldn't let us forget it.   (I always wondered why "youse guys" was more acceptable than "you all.") I pretty much went into homesickness right away, which is a form of depression.   I expected that, but as I got into the swing of things I became more and more depressed.   I was suicidal, unhappy at being at the school, scared, and frantic at how unhappy I was.   This was not how I had envisioned my time at college.   Again, I stopped sleeping, usually operating on around three to four hours sleep.   I simply didn't want to be at this school and I let everyone know how unhappy I was.

The nuns who ran the school were much more conservative than I was used to.   Our education was to be more religion-oriented than I was expecting, and even worse, most of the students were much behind where I had been at high school graduation.   Most of my classes were remedial, going over the same things I had learned my junior and senior years in high school.   I remember an orientation meeting, in which we were told that we were to be educated to be "Senator's wives." I piped up and asked, "What if we want to be Senators?" This, needless to say, did not go over well.   They were going to teach us to be ladies, and I was determined to fight that all the way.   I did not want to go to a finishing school, which is how they saw themselves in many ways, but to an intellectual center.

As an example of their rigidity, all freshmen were required to go to choir practice the first four weeks of school so we could learn the hymns sung at the school during religious services.   One of our number, Kathy, whom I didn't know at the time, but who later became a friend, was tone-deaf.   The nun leading the choir immediately detected her off-key singing and ordered her to stop.   After choir, Kathy told her that she wasn't going to come to choir practice if she wasn't going to be allowed to sing.   She was told if she didn't come she would receive the same punishment as the rest of us who chose not to come to choir -- restriction to campus for the entire weekend.   However, she would still not be allowed to sing.   She didn't go to choir and spent the first month on campus. I always admired her for that.

We had "mixers" with the boys from the boys' school from across town. I went to these and enjoyed them, but wasn't much interested in dating. I was still going with Glenn, the guy from the wrong side of the tracks in Oklahoma whom I had dated in high school The other girls seem determined to get hooked up as soon as possible.

In a science class, a nun answered a question by saying, "Because that's how God made it." I was horrified. I thought, again, that I had come to college to learn and was given an answer that a six-year old would be satisfied with in first grade if he or she weren't too bright. In medieval history, I was learning the "Catholic" version of European history, which certainly skewed the story. English was a rehash of my junior year in high school. Philosophy was Catholic doctrine. A nun actually answered a question by saying, "You can't think that." (The only response to that is, of course, to keep your mouth shut but to know that you can think anything you want. They can't take away your mind, hard as they may try.) The only class I enjoyed or got anything out of was my government class. Robert Henry taught me all I know about practical politics, and changed my minor from English to political science. I suffered through my other classes, bored and becoming more and more depressed.

I read the "Kansas City Star" in the library every day, and was interested in a story that the first Mensa Chapter in the area was being organized. It explained that Mensa was a social group for people who scored in the top two percent of the population in IQ scores. I was interested in joining, after being told in high school I was in the top two percent of the population in IQ scores. I thought I might find some like-minded people in such a group, but had no way to get to Kansas City for testing or to attend meetings, so soon forgot about it.

Because of my depression, I couldn't sleep or eat or concentrate, and while, given the circumstances, I should have been making straight As, I was pulling down Bs. I didn't feel accepted by these Midwestern girls, who kept insisting that I was racially prejudiced. Most of them came from all-white towns and didn't have a clue, but they knew that since I was from Oklahoma, I was prejudiced. They couldn't have known, and weren't interested in knowing, that we had a heck of a time arranging our senior events in high school because we were one of the first racially integrated graduating classes in the city. I had the job of finding places that would accept our class for activities and it was, indeed, frustrating. Most of the places senior classes went to for final-year activities were closed to us, and we refused to go anywhere where all of us were not welcome.

But things got worse. On top of what I considered rigid and intrusive rules of conduct and unresponsive and inappropriate education, I learned about Midwestern weather. My parents had never lived north of Oklahoma, and had sent me to school with a hat, coat, and a pair of gloves, which would get me through the worst of central Oklahoma weather. We didn't know that somewhere between Oklahoma City and Kansas City the climate completely changed. I learned that at the first snowfall, which happened in October, for heaven's sake. It snowed and snowed. The nuns didn't believe it was ladylike for women to wear pants, so we weren't allowed to. I froze in my ladylike skirts. The other girls were prepared with knee socks, but I had never seen them before. I put in an urgent request for knee socks for Christmas.

And still it snowed and the temperature dropped. It was often 10 or 15 degrees below zero, which was colder than I had ever experienced. The snow was several feet deep, which was also new to me. What was worse was that none of us had cars so we had to walk everywhere. I was so cold. I just couldn't get warm. I caught several bad colds and couldn't shake them. They turned into sinus infections, which I had never experienced before. I stayed sick most of the time. The skin peeled off my legs where it had frozen. I was miserable. No one at school understood why I was so unhappy. This did not improve my mood at all.

Just before Thanksgiving vacation, President Kennedy was assassinated. Just like everyone else of my age, I remember exactly where I was when I heard the news. It fell to Bob Henry to try to comfort us. It was the most shocking thing that had ever happened in my life; nothing in public life ever shocked me as much again. The whole country shut down for mourning and for the funeral; we were sent home early for Thanksgiving to grieve with our families after a student committed suicide the day after the assassination. It was all horrible. Nothing would be the same for us again; and indeed, it hasn't.

My mood was also not improved by word filtering back to me that my Oklahoma City boyfriend, Glenn, was running around with one of my girlfriends from home. I dealt with that when I returned home for Christmas, but never felt good about our relationship after that and ended it a few weeks later. I remember being terribly depressed over Christmas, not helped by the fact that my bedroom was now inhabited by a foster sister taken in by my mother after my departure, and my elderly cat, who nearly staved to death after I left, had dealt with his grief by completely forgetting who I was! However, it did get me over any residual homesickness. My mother continued to take in foster children as her own children left home. We soon got used to it; it was just a little startling the first time. Her philosophy was "I have an empty bed and there are children out there who don't have beds." A good thing was that I got my braces taken off during the break.

By February I had recovered enough to meet and start dating Maurice. He was a freshman at the boys' school and it just pleased everyone that I was dating a nice Catholic boy. I wasn't so sure that I was as pleased as everyone else, but my friends and parents seemed to think that he was the best thing for me. I survived the first year.

CHAPTER 10: THERE ARE MONSTERS

The summer of '64 I spent working as a file clerk in the billing office of St. Anthony's Hospital, only a few blocks from my home and the hospital where I was born. I had worked in a cafeteria and in a restaurant previously, but all these jobs did for me was to convince me that I needed to finish college. I wanted a job that allowed me more autonomy than any of these did. I also enjoyed a lot of time at an underage teen club, dancing and meeting guys and dating. The big song that summer was "Oh, Pretty Woman," by Roy Orbison and I can never hear it without thinking of that summer. My mother was horrified. She was so happy with my relationship with Maurice, she was ready for the wedding already. I wasn't. The work allowed me to save up spending money for school. I would also have to have a job at school my sophomore year, because my sister was starting college in Wichita that year.

So when I arrived at school, I was able to get a 20-hour a week job working in the library. I knew then that the schoolwork was not as difficult as I thought it would be when I entered college, so signed up for 19 hours. All of the drawbacks I have found in the school the previous year were still present, but at least this time they weren't a surprise. And I had a good supply of knee socks so I wouldn't freeze to death, even though this winter we were to suffer through a six-week period of the temperature never going above 32 degrees.

Sometime during the year, I finally lost patience with the far right wing editor of the town newspaper. He constantly railed at the federal government for its free hand with federal aid and government assistance. I sent a letter to the editor, pointing out that a few years before, the town had been underwater as a result of a flood on the Missouri River, and that if it had not been for federal aid, the town would still be, both literally and figuratively, six feet under. I didn't realize that I should have asked permission of the powers that be at school before I sent the letter; silly me, I thought it was my right to express a political opinion. I set off a firestorm of criticism aimed at me: didn't I realize that I had hurt town-gown relationships? Didn't I realize that it wasn't my place to criticize how the town ran itself? One nun quietly took me aside and told me she thought I was right, but didn't defend me in public. I honestly had no idea that a letter to the editor was controversial. It showed me again how separate I was from the rest of the students and how far I was from the value system of the college. I was no lady, and here I was in a finishing school for young ladies..

I had a boyfriend, Maurice, who was every girl's dream in terms of attentiveness, politeness, and romance. The major problem was that, for me, the chemistry just wasn't there. I had made such a mess of my previous relationships and everyone kept telling me how lucky I was, so I hung in, trying to believe that he was for me. In the fall, he surprised me by getting tickets for us to see the Oklahoma University-Kansas State University football game. I sent a telegram to Jim to let him know I'd be in the stands, and was more excited to see him play than to be with Maury. I didn't try to see Jim after the game because I could see it would not be a good idea. But it reminded me that I still felt more for Jim than I did for Maury. I was carrying a torch for a guy who was married to someone else and I hadn't seen for a couple of years, so how could I possibly be in love with Maury? None of it felt right. And, again, I was operating in depression.

I found that my illness, though definitely present, stayed more under control the busier I was. Taking 19 hours, working 20 hours a week, and dating regularly kept me busy and more on an even keel, though I am sure I had my ups and downs. Later, a social worker advised me to always keep busy if I felt I was slipping. I have found her advice to be excellent. If you stop to worry about your mood, you soon succumb to it.

My parents were beginning to learn that adult children sometimes do not do what they wanted them to do -- sometime that winter my brother dropped out of the seminary, thus destroying my mother's dream of his being a priest. With no money and no where to go, he returned home to work on a Masters' at Oklahoma City University. My father insisted that he prove he was a real man, so even though he had been injured and had surgery recently, he had to work on a construction site to earn money to pay rent to stay at home.

I was not any happier with the education I was receiving or with my relationship with Maury. In March , for my birthday, he took me home to meet his parents. It was a total disaster from my point of view. For one thing, it was spring in my way of calculating these things, but our train got stuck in a snow bank overnight and when we got to the small Iowa town he lived in, the ground was buried under six feet of snow.

If my mother had been meeting my fiancé for the first time, she would have, as she later did, pull out the good china and crystal and prepare a fantastic meal. I was served hot dogs on paper plates by his parents. The atmosphere was obviously chilly (not just from the weather), and he later explained that his family was not certain that I (being from Oklahoma and all) was of a high enough social class to marry their son. This made me even more wary of the relationship, but still, I continued to hang in. I didn't want to disappoint anyone. Again, I was depressed and didn't know how to get off dead center.

After we returned from the trip, Maurice sat down and explained how it would be after we got married. He had talked with his parents, and his father had agreed to send me to law school, so we would go to law school together after we were married. Then we would return to the small town he was from, move in with his parents since they had such

55

a large home, take over his father's law practice, and I could take over his mother's place as head of the garden and art clubs. He would, of course, give me a generous allowance for clothing and to run my part of the house.

I don't remember saying anything. I was more or less in shock. I had always wanted to go to law school, but never, in my wildest imaginings, had I wound up in a small Iowa town, freezing in the winter, trying to be the social leader of said town while living as a dependent in my in-law's home. I was flabbergasted that I had not even been consulted before any of these plans were made. I felt bonds of barbed wire tightening all around me. I knew how unhappy everyone would be if I broke up with him, and he certainly hadn't given me a reason to break up, but I was one unhappy person.

One thing I had become sure of, and that was I had begun to see no value in virginity. I was tired of not doing something, and could see no reason to spend years refusing to have sex. As the school year drew to a close, I asked Maury, "Couldn't you buy a condom and we go to St. Joseph (Missouri) some Friday night and rent a motel room?" He said, "No, we should wait until we're married. That's the right thing to do." Well, we wouldn't be married for another year and a half, and I was tired of celibacy. I really saw no reason to go on with a relationship that I was getting little out of if I couldn't even have sex. I left school that summer, relieved that I had made it through another year, but not looking forward to another.

CHAPTER 11: There Are Angels

I was poised for changed by the summer of 1965. I tried to find a job, but could not. I decided to take a class rather than just sit around all summer. I enrolled in a government course at the University of Oklahoma, was able to find a ride, and secured a job on campus working in the science library. I was a little shocked at my salary, because at the Mount I had received $1.25 an hour, which was minimum wage then. At the University, I got $.80 an hour. And that was the prevailing wage all over Norman, Oklahoma, the town OU was in. Base salary for every job, including city jobs, was $.80 per hour. It did you no good to look for work off-campus, because your job would pay the same all over town. The money would pay my commuting costs and allow some spending money, and that was about it. I wouldn't be able to save a lot of it.

My professor at OU was John Paul Duncan, who, as it turned out, was world-renowned in his field of comparative government and the best teacher I ever had in any subject, bar none. He taught all over the world, spending every third year at Cambridge. He was an excellent teacher, who loved teaching and students. I was amazed at both the freedom of thought and speech in his class, and the way he encouraged us to express ourselves. The atmosphere was intellectual, and he did his best to get us to stretch our minds and to think for ourselves. I loved the class and felt like I had finally found college. I wanted to transfer right then to the University, but of course my parents wouldn't hear of it, and I wouldn't be 21 until March of the next year.

One of the students in the class was Eddie, whom I started spending a lot of time with. He was a grad student in history and I was flattered that he was interested in me. He was so interested in me, in fact, that after a month of dating he finally removed that disability, my virginity. We talked of marriage, and when Maurice came for his visit to me and my parents in August, I broke up with him without a regret. I was so pleased with the school, with Eddie, and with my life that my mood had flip-flopped and I was manic again. I couldn't see why everything wouldn't work out great.

I just assumed that, having slept with Eddie, he would be the man I would marry. We spent all our time together that summer after school was out. He lived on the same street I did, only a few blocks away. Neither of us had any money, but we still managed to have fun running around with his friends. Eddie had an ambition, though, that was going to interrupt his education. He wanted to travel around the world. First he would drive me back to school in the fall, then he would take off on his 'round-the-world odyssey. He wouldn't return until I graduated.

Before I went back to school, my mother talked with me. I'll never forget that conversation. I was sitting on the kitchen stairs. She said, "You know that your brother (who was now at DePaul University) is in school and we feel that we need to help him because it is more important that a man get an education than a woman. Also, your sister does not want to go back to school because she doesn't have new clothes to wear so we've decided to buy her a new wardrobe to go back to school in. So this year, we aren't going to give you any help at all. You will have to pay for it yourself. We know that you want to go to school so badly that you'll figure out a way to do it."

I was speechless. I couldn't think of a thing to say. Later, I found out that my sister really didn't want to go back to school and the clothes thing was an excuse -- she expected them to let her off the hook if she demanded new clothes. I just went up to my room and started packing. So, for my junior year, I went off to the school I hated with a scholarship, a job, a loan and what little spending money I had saved from the summer.

At least I was able to get them to let Eddie drive me to school. We managed it so that we could spend the night together before he dropped me off. I had never spent the night with a man before so it was a new experience. It was also eye-opening. The first thing he did after he opened his eyes in the morning was to pick up the flat, warm bottle of beer he was drinking the night before and take a swig. This set off all kinds of warnings in my head. I knew he always carried around a quart of beer, but I thought he was nursing the same bottle for hours. There were no alcoholics in my immediate family, but so many in my extended family that it caused me to take a step back and be just a little more cautious.

School was even worse this year. Maurice was a popular guy and everyone let me know how unpopular I was for dumping him. He was not hostile, but his friends were, openly. One of them told everyone I was a pathological liar; for example, how could someone from Oklahoma City have ever met the Four Preps? And being from Oklahoma, how could I have met the All-American fullback, Jim, who, though he played for OU, was from Texas? I couldn't defend myself, everyone by then agreed I was lying.

While I was being cut dead socially, I also didn't hear a word from Eddie. Not a postcard, not a phone call. I began to feel like an idiot, like I had really been taken in. I spent Thanksgiving with some distant cousins in Leavenworth, because my parents said they didn't have the money for me to come home. While I was there, someone from the school forwarded my first letter from Eddie to my cousins.' home. I was absolutely thrilled to hear from him; he was in Samoa and having a great time. There was no explanation as to why it had taken him three months to write, but I was so happy to hear from him I didn't even care. I had flip-flopped into depression again, and his letter pulled me out of it to a degree.

School continued as it always had. I had a science requirement, so I had enrolled in a genetics class to fulfill it. Genetics was a new science at the time; Watson and Crick had described the double helix only a few years before. There were new and exciting discoveries being made constantly; the science was exploding. I was completely fascinated by it. We were required to do a certain amount of outside reading besides our textbook; books were placed on reserve in the library with selections we could choose to read. I read it all. What I was learning in genetics was confirming my world view that life was basically random. I made 100 percent on all the tests and carried the highest average in the class, beating out all the science majors. I really took the class seriously. For our final exam, we were to make up an outline of the important topics of the subject and discuss them in class. My outline was five pages long and I was loaded for bear.

One topic we had not touched on in class, but I was really interested in was sort of a dream of geneticists then -- a reality now -- that a fetus could have genetic problems corrected in utero and be born whole. As soon as there was an opportunity , I brought the topic up, to be told, "If God wants children to be born defective, then we should have defective children." It was like a slap in the face. I had been so excited by the new ideas, by the new science that I had forgotten who I was talking to. I was floored. I shut my mouth for the rest of the class, took my A, and wondered how I would ever be able to return to the school after the holidays. I would be turning 21 in 10 weeks; perhaps I would not.

CHAPTER 12: THERE'S A PEACEFULNESS

When I went home for the Christmas holidays, I was discouraged and lonely. I just didn't see how I could continue at a place that was so different from me in philosophy and where I was so shunned. On top of that, the man I loved was half a world away and, again, I hadn't heard from him since that one letter at Thanksgiving. There was no present from him under the tree.

A couple of evenings after returning home, I looked idly out of my bedroom window and saw Eddie's car pull up in front of my house. I don't believe that I have ever been so surprised or happy before or since in my life. I tried to run downstairs in just a slip, but was stopped by my father, who insisted I dress. I hurriedly slipped into a dress and ran down the stairs and into Eddie's arms. I think it is the only time in my life I have cried for joy. He explained that he had just missed me so much he decided to come home. He said, "Let's get married." Startled, I said, "When?" "Next week," he answered. Again, warning bells went off and I asked him why he wanted to get married so soon. "Well, you can go to work to support us and I'll work on my doctorate." I told him that I had no intention of dropping out of school or getting married until I had my degree, but that I would transfer to Oklahoma University so I could be close to him.

This time my parents couldn't talk me out of transferring. I was determined to do so and they would have to go along. OU was not on the same schedule as the Mount; their second semester didn't start until the middle of February. So I notified my roommate at the Mount and she packed my things. Eddie and I drove up there for the last time and I shook the Kansas dirt from my feet.

Not knowing how to transfer to OU, I just drove there one afternoon and walked into the head of the history department's office. No one was around because it was between semesters. I found a man in jeans and cowboy boots reading the newspaper and asked, "Where can I find the head of the department?" He lowered the paper, looked over it at me, and said, "You've found him." This was Arrell Morgan Gibson, who would have a profound effect on my education. He took the time to listen to my story, to go over my transcript with me, and to plan out a schedule for the next semester for me. He got me the papers, including an application for a scholarship, told me the nuts and bolts of what I would need to do to transfer and generally went out of his way to make sure I understood what was necessary.

My parents, of course, were unhappy with my decision. I would have to depend on them for tuition and book money, but it was so much cheaper than the Mount I couldn't see that it would be much of a problem. (A semester of tuition and fees for OU was around $200 at that time.) I got my old job at the science library back, and through a friend of Eddie's, found a really small, firetrap of an apartment only a half-block off campus. The rent was only $40 a month, so I would pay for rent and food with my earnings. (My job paid around $70 a month). I was set.

I was so pleased to have a place of my own for the first time in my life. Of course it was really not a nice place -- it was broiling hot in the summer and really cold in the winter; it was tiny and the furnishings were hand-me-down college student. But it was mine; and for the first time, I could shut the world out. I had been surrounded by people all my life and had always wanted to live alone, just to know what it was like. And, for the first time on a Sunday morning, I woke up and decided that I didn't have to go to Mass. And didn't. I rolled over and went back to sleep. I never did went to church again unless it was for a wedding or funeral.

Of course, I didn't own a single pair of jeans -- just sweaters and skirts, and I didn't have a car. But what I did have was the feeling of freedom, and the willingness to go without almost everything to have freedom of thought and speech. When I presented the admission papers to my parents to sign, (I wouldn't be 21 for another three weeks) my mother signed and took them to my father. I heard him say, "I'm not signing these -- I don't approve of her going to school there and I don't have to give permission." My mother said, "You'll sign or you'll never see her again!"

Mother knew how serious I was and that I was going to go to OU. She knew that I would not forgive them if they made me lose a semester because I was three weeks short of my birthday. When classes started, I knew I had not made a mistake. The freedom, the openness, the intellectual curiosity were exactly what I had been wanting for the past two and a half years. I had never been happier. And I wasn't depressed any longer; I was manic again -- I had the world by the tail and could accomplish anything. I was just where I wanted to be and nothing was going to stop me.

My second month there, there was a computer glitch and the students who worked on campus didn't get their checks. We were paid only once a month and all of us who depended on campus jobs were broke. I didn't have anything to eat. I hung around the student union where friends bought me coffee and, once or twice, a sandwich. Had I been at school longer, I would have known that I could have gone to the University President's house, only a couple of blocks from mine, and he would have given me food. George Cross was a sympathetic and good administrator. As it was, I toughed it out for the three days it took to get the computer up.

While working at the library one day, I picked up a student directory and idly looked at it. To my great surprise, Jim's name was in it. I called his number, and he came over to the library to talk. He hadn't been able to finish his degree because of all the football, then, he had played some pro ball. Now, he was back for a semester to finish up. It was great talking to him and catching up. I had thought I would never see him again so this was a bonus.

However, things were not going swimmingly with Eddie. I had started paying attention to his drinking, and found that he was downing quart after quart of beer. He drank constantly. Once, when he was in a situation where he couldn't drink, he became testy, then spent several hours in a bar making up for lost time. Of course, I was bored sitting in the bar, and started wondering if I wanted to spend future years like that. Then, I discovered that he had made a girl in Samoa pregnant. I suspected that was his reason for coming home so abruptly. When I confronted him about it, he said, "Well, she's only a native girl." He said he did not plan to support the child or ever even see it. This did not impress me. I also noted that he did not seem to be making progress on his PhD. By the end of the spring semester, I had been awarded a tuition scholarship to OU, had 16 more hours under my belt, and was happier with my education than ever before. I had also dumped Eddie.

CHAPTER 13: AND A RAGE
INSIDE US ALL

By the summer of '66, I was way manic. I didn't know it then. I just knew I had the world by the tail and everything was going my way. In one way, it was good because I took a heavy load that summer semester. I had lost eleven hours because OU wouldn't, of course, accept my religious instruction hours. Plus, I had some requirements to get out of the way. OU required Arts and Sciences students to take geology, and I needed to start my education courses if I were to be teacher-certified. So, that summer, I took both a geology and an education course. It required me to be in two classes four days a week and two labs a week for geology. I also, of course, had to work. The classes were early, because none of the classrooms were air-conditioned.

I loved geology because the teacher told us great World War II stories from his experiences and took us on a field trip to the Arbuckle Mountains so we could see what we had been learning in class. Geology was fascinating and it was nice to have a break from the social sciences for a time.

Meanwhile, I was dating Terry, Steve, Lyle and Ron -- and sleeping with all of them. (With careful birth-control, of course). Hallmark symptoms of bipolar disorder are hyper sexuality and promiscuity. I didn't know that, of course, I just thought that I was looking for the right guy while having a good time. I felt absolutely no guilt and didn't worry about it. Of course, there was no AIDS to concern us at that time. I really didn't feel anything for any of them except Ron. It just seemed like the thing to do. Ron had signed up for the Navy and was waiting to be inducted; in those Vietnam years, there was a long line of men trying to get in the Navy. He left at the end of the summer school. I would miss him, and we stayed in touch during his basic training. He visited once before he shipped out.

In August, after summer school, Norman became a ghost town. Only one grocery store and restaurant stayed open; the others closed until school started again in September. They alternated each year. Only a few students stayed in town; I was one of them because I had to work to pay my rent. My mother had asked me to come home for the month, but I told her I had to pay my rent for August. She didn't offer to pay the rent, so I knew I hadn't been forgiven yet. Norman had only about 12,000 residents then; the school had a population of 20,000. During this time, I met and started dating Bill. He had just come back from a two-year stint in the Army. He'd been drafted and he fully expected to be sent to Vietnam and to serve as cannon fodder, but after his IQ test, the Army had sent him to Germany to work with nuclear missiles. We had a month to get to know one another with no school, so we spent a lot of time together.

Bill had a wicked sense of humor that drew me to him immediately, absolutely no money except for the G.I.Bill (which meant he had a lot more than I did), and was obviously bright. We got along well, but as I learned more about his situation, I became disillusioned with him. He told me that he had managed to rack up 42 hours of F during his years at OU before he went to the Army, and had "earned" another 6 in summer school that had just ended. He had thrown away a full scholarship his freshman year and would lose his G.I. Bill if this continued. He wanted to continue our relationship in the fall, but I told him that I was concentrating on school and simply didn't have time for someone who didn't take it seriously. Obviously, he didn't study and all he would do is drag me down with him. So I was not interested in seeing him anymore.

He said, "Please help me. I never studied in high school and I've never learned to study. I need someone to show me how." I was dubious. Forty-eight hours of F would require him to make 48 hours of A, or a proportionally larger number of Bs to bring his average up to a C so he could graduate. It was a tremendous task and I frankly didn't believe that he had the moxie to do it. But I said I would help him get started for the fall semester. When school started, I made sure he had all his books and a notebook for each class. Then every night I took him to the library with me. Eventually he caught on, learned the knack of taking good notes in class, and began to do better.

Meanwhile, things were looking up for me. Dr. Gibson got me a job in the Western History division of the library paying $1.25 an hour. I had caught up my hours, so only had to take 15 this semester, all social sciences. It was a lot of reading and writing, but nothing difficult. By the end of the semester, I had done well, and Bill had made all As and Bs. We were a couple by then.

By the start of the spring semester, Bill's living arrangements had ended and he needed a place to live; I let him move in with me. Unmarried couples did not live together in the mid-sixties, at least not in Oklahoma, but it seemed natural for him to move in with me, since he didn't have any other place to go. My last semester was a tough one in that I had found that I needed two more hours of a foreign language to graduate; the only course open was a Spanish composition class. I had never done well in Spanish, it was just something I had to get through. Bill's grades were staying up.

I spoke to Dr. Gibson about continuing on in graduate school after I graduated. Bill was not even close to graduating and there wasn't much else for me to do in Norman. Women didn't go to graduate school at that time; in fact women didn't do a lot of things. Bill was an engineering student and there was only one female in his whole school. He reported that she was the object of ridicule and hazing, even from some professors. Dr. Gibson was surprisingly open; he told me that he would sponsor me in his program and handed me some papers to fill out.

I later found out that Dr. Gibson had two daughters in high school who, he had realized, would not be able to follow in his footsteps, so he had decided to sponsor two females for their Masters Degree every year, and allow one to go on for her Doctorate. He was the only professor in the history department who took women. One of the papers he handed me was an application for a scholarship. It was a simple, one-page document that was a grant to pay all expenses for a Masters Degree, including books. I was accepted for grad school and for the grant.

At some point in this period Bill and I had a fight, and I said something like, "And I thought you would be the one I would marry." He took that as a proposal and suddenly we were planning on getting married. We got on well and I really liked him. I didn't feel about him as I had about Jim, but I had decided that Jim as a once-in-a-lifetime thing and I just shouldn't expect it. At first we thought we would get married at the end of the semester, after I graduated, but then we realized that I would be starting grad school only a few days after that, so we decided to have the ceremony over spring break. One of the reasons we decided to go ahead and marry was that our parents kept dropping in on us unannounced and we had to pretend we were not living together; another was that the G.I.Bill would go from $100 a month to $125. It seemed that it would make life much simpler. Also, and this was a major reason I agreed to get married, I was afraid of facing the world alone, with no money and no job after graduation. What would I do? Where would I go? Perhaps if I had been able to type, I would have taken off for Washington, DC, but a woman had to be able to type to get just about any kind of job except teaching. I knew I couldn't return to my parent's home, and I had no money, no car, no job.

When we told my parents, they were happy. They liked Bill, and felt that he would be a good son-in-law. I believe that they were glad that

I was "finally" settling down. When we told Bill's mother she said, "Well, I guess you wouldn't be marrying her if she wasn't pregnant." That set the tone for my relationship with my mother-in-law for my whole marriage. I had seen my mother, whose mother-in-law lived with her for thirty years get along beautifully with all her in-laws and actually thought mother-in-law jokes were jokes. I was to quickly learn differently.

I didn't want to change my name when I got married -- I liked my own name better than his. I ran the idea past him, and he said, "But that would embarrass me." When I found out that the law required I would still have to vote under his name, I decided to go all the way and change my name to his.

We planned a simple wedding, partly because we were in school and partly because I didn't want my father involved in any way; I had a vivid memory of his behavior at my older sister's wedding. We soon learned that no matter what we did, we couldn't make anyone happy. We made plans to get married in the Newman chapel in Norman, mainly to please my parents. Bill's parents hadn't been to church in years, so he thought they would be fine with it. However, they told him that if he got married in a Catholic Church they wouldn't attend. It was the last time he chose his mother over me. He told them he'd "miss them." They decided to come. Meanwhile, my family was unhappy that I was not having a Mass at the wedding.

I decided to not have showers because they would interfere with midterms, but my aunt scheduled one without my knowledge. That made my mother-in-law angry, so she scheduled one, too.

It made me sad when a drunk Eddie called me the week before the wedding, dropping coins all over the floor of the phone booth, wanting to get back together. I gave him the news that I was getting married and told him it was definitely too late.

We bought plain wedding bands on time -- they cost us $60. My mother insisted on a new dress, and she bought me a beige suit with matching shoes. We hadn't planned on a reception, but my mother planned a small one at a restaurant. Instead of being something we could slide into, we were exhausted by the wedding, what with showers and midterms. I chose a friend to stand up for me, because I couldn't choose between my sisters. Bill had his best friend come in from Chicago. His friend, as it turned out was Jewish, and Jews cannot be best men at a Catholic wedding. I told them to keep their mouths shut and we went on with it.

The actual wedding went off without a hitch on March 27, 1967, and was really nice. The spring weather was perfect. The church was filled with flowers because it was the day after Easter. The priest, Father Naberhaus, refused a remuneration for performing the ceremony because he knew we didn't have much money. We hadn't planned a honeymoon, but Bill's parents gave us money for a short getaway. We quickly chose a resort, and headed out in a borrowed car.

CHAPTER 14: THERE IS SUGAR

I was optimistic (manic) when I married. I really thought marriage would fix me, settle me down, stop my moods from fluctuating. Like so many others before me, I found that nothing changed within me. I brought all my problems to the marriage, and no matter how much I wanted to succeed, I was going to have to live with who I was. Bill had always wanted a lot of sex, and I assumed that was normal for a courtship phase. However, on our honeymoon night he wanted sex six times, even after I told him I was tired and sore and not at all interested in more sex. He kept after me until I did what he wanted. At the same time, my mood plummeted. By morning, I felt I had made a huge mistake and that I shouldn't have gone through with it. His attitude toward me had definitely changed; now I was property, he could do with me as he wished. I felt that I was married and had to live with it.

Even with the problems that Bill and I had, I do not think that a marriage with anyone would have succeeded. I was too restless, had mood swings, and used poor judgment way too often for a marriage to work out. In addition to that, there was my upbringing, which taught me that you live with what hand you are dealt. I did not speak up for my-self when I should have, but blew up when I couldn't take it anymore.

Graduation, a few weeks later was an anticlimax, except for the suspense over my Spanish grade. If I failed, I'd lose my scholarship and have to take another language class in summer school to graduate. My teacher was kind enough to call and let me know that I had squeaked by with a "D," the only one I ever made but one which made me happy.

We celebrated graduation by moving into student housing, which was old Navy Bachelor's Officers' Quarters left over from World War II. I thought they were wonderful after what I had lived in before; mean-while, my new next-door neighbor wept because they were so tacky. We would still have to go the library to study in air-conditioning, but neither of us had been raised with air conditioning, so it didn't bother us so much.

Shortly before we were married, I visited the Student Medical Service to obtain birth control pills. Since I was over 21, I didn't think it would be a problem, and it certainly wasn't. OU had a student die due to an illegal abortion only a couple of months before, and they were happy to supply birth control to anyone who asked. However, I did learn more about my husband. I developed a migraine with the first month's dose. Unfortunately, it happened at a drive-in movie, where they were show-ing several movies Bill wanted to see. He refused to go home when I told him I was sick, and finally left angrily when I started to cry from the pain during the third feature. He didn't seem to care how I felt; he was just upset because I had ruined his evening. The next month the dosage was adjusted and the pills actually made me feel better than I ever had.

We took out a modest student loan to pay our rent because I wouldn't be able to work in grad school and Bill was still trying to keep his grades as high as possible. We lived on the G.I. Bill, not well but adequately. I learned to cook hamburger every way there was, and there was always fried chicken. We ate out rarely. These were not liberated times; I did all the housework. To unwind from studying, we took long walks. You would be amazed at how much money you can find on the ground if you keep your eyes open; if we found a dime, we split a coke. If we found a quarter, we could play pinball. That was our amusement; we had no money for other activities.

Six weeks after our wedding, I called Jim when he came into town for the alumni football game. Not even marriage had changed my feelings for him. We chatted briefly, again catching up on each other's lives. I didn't suggest that Bill and I go to the game; I knew that he would know how I felt.

Grad school turned out to be harder than I expected. Summer school was especially rough, and at one point I broke down and cried, saying that I just couldn't do it. But I pulled it together and got everything done on time. I learned that you could not procrastinate and you had to stay on top of things to make certain all the deadlines were met. I think that is one of the most important things I took away from grad school -- it helped me later in my jobs. I worked with many others who had never learned this lesson.

Outside of sex problems -- Bill always demanding sex no matter how I felt -- and my restlessness, we did well together as students. Our goals were the same and we worked well together to reach them. For his social science requirement, Bill signed up for advanced history courses so he could take them with me and did fine in them. His engineering courses were going well, too. I signed up for every course I could with Professors Duncan and Gibson, even though they were hard teachers who required a lot. After the lackadaisical education I had received at the Mount, I felt that I ought to take every opportunity to learn as much as I could.

I received my MA in June of 1968. Bill had taken enough courses to get his degree, but had not yet raised his grade-point average to a "C." I began taking more education courses so I could eventually be certified as a high school teacher, though my goal was to teach in junior college, while he took advanced engineering courses in the field of electronics communications.

We didn't know when he would graduate because, until he got his grades each semester, we didn't know what his grade-point average would be. Finally, in December of 1968, things were looking like he would pull it off. He sent off resumes to places he would like to work, and I waited to see where we would end up. At the time, I was hoping for Los Angeles or Seattle, because I wanted to be as far away from our families as we could get. As it was, a company in Dallas hired him, sight unseen, and offered to pay for out move down there. It was the best and only deal we were offered, so, reluctantly on my part, we were off to Dallas as soon as the grades were in and it was obvious he had attained, finally, a "C" average.

CHAPTER 15: AND THERE IS SALT

Dallas was a small southern city when we moved there, half its present size, and not the trendy, sophisticated city it is now. We rented an apartment down the road from Bill's job, the first one we found that would accept pets, because I really wanted a kitten. Snowball was 21 years old, I felt too old to move from my parents' home. Besides, he really seemed to have forgotten who I was. The apartment was in the Oak Cliff section of Dallas, which was not the most desirable area, but we didn't know that. I started looking for work, and to learn my way around town, I took temporary work and rode the buses.

Bill really didn't care much for his job, which was testing electronic equipment for fighter jets, but it paid well and gave him some experience. Meanwhile, I still didn't have a teaching certificate and had come in the wrong time of the year to look for a teaching position. I applied for Federal jobs, but found that even with an MA, I had to take a typing test. I asked if men were also given typing tests, but was never even graced with a reply. As I learned my way around, I applied for state jobs, too, and was hired in July of 1969 as a Child Welfare caseworker. At that time, there were no requirements for a caseworker except a college degree.

My start date was a little weird, because I was due to start on the morning after the moon landing, and all employees were given the day off. So my first day was a holiday. Bill and I bought a television for the occasion. We hadn't had one in school because we thought it would distract from school and studying, but this occasion demanded one. We figured the only things we had missed by not having one were the television coverage of the Bobby Kennedy and Martin Luther King, Jr. assassinations. (I've never seen an episode of "Gilligan's Island," but don't feel that I have missed much.) We stayed up most of the night with the rest of the country to see Armstrong step onto the moon.

I was assigned to foster homes. My supervisor, Jackie, was to become the best and closest friend I ever had. She was an understanding, loving person who took the thankless job of finding homes for abused and neglected children seriously. The job was impossible. There were simply not enough eligible homes and we were forced to break licensing regulations left and right to place children. Fragile children would die in hospitals or institutions; it was better to crowd them a little in foster homes than to ignore them in institutions. We were always being begged by workers for one more placement, and begging foster parents to take one more child. ("No baby bed? You do have a laundry basket, don't you? Well, that will be okay.") We had neither the money nor the resources to do a halfway decent job, but we did our best.

In January of 1969, with both of us working, Bill and I bought a cute little house in a nice part of town. I also needed a car for my work. Bill picked it out, and since I had asked for a green one, he came home with a red Camaro. I don't know what it is with men and red cars, but I drove a car whose color I hated for the next eight years. It was while I was working at Child Welfare that I did something that illustrates the colossal bad judgment that a person with bipolar disorder can exercise.

I drove to Oklahoma City to see my parents and to meet Bill, who was going to come there after a business trip to Florida. The trip, however, lasted longer than he had thought so I returned home with a side trip through Norman. There I picked up a couple of student hitchhikers, drove them to Dallas, and allowed them to use the house for a weekend while I flew to Florida to join Bill on his trip. I didn't know their names or where they lived.

When we returned home, there was evidence of the house being used and he asked me what had happened. I told him and he was, of course, aghast. I couldn't explain, and didn't understand, why I had done such a thing. It simply -- and this is the mantra of the person with bipolar disorder -- seemed like a good idea at the time. When manic, it doesn't seem like anything bad can happen. Everything you do will turn out okay, no matter how stupid it is, even if it is illegal. There is no thought before action. You just do it and assume it will turn out. Therefore, it is impossible to explain it to someone else. Luckily, the house was not trashed and nothing had been stolen. I got away with it that time, but it could have been disastrous.

About a year into the position at Child Welfare, a worker discovered that a political appointee had beaten children in the county children's shelter. I was burned out by then, supported well by my husband, and so was one of those who was able to go public to demand the firing of this woman and better conditions at the shelter. Nothing changed, but I lost my job, as I expected to. We made plans to try to have a child, which I was halfway reconciled to.

Ten days later, Bill was suddenly laid off. I went back on birth control pills, and we both started looking for jobs. Neither of us could find anything immediately, so we both enrolled in school, Bill to work on his Masters and me to get my teaching certificate. I found a program that would allow me to finish in only one semester, and Bill found a math teaching job in a private school that would help pay expenses.

CHAPTER 16: There Is Ice

I tried to talk with Bill about our sex problem, but he couldn't seem to hear me. He wanted sex at least once a day, but usually more. I couldn't get out of bed on Saturday or Sunday without having sex, and I soon learned to change clothes in the bathroom with the door shut because if he saw me with my clothes off he had to have sex, no matter what else was happening. Even if we had plans to go out, he would want me to stop and have sex with him, or if I was changing after a hard day's work in preparation to cook dinner. If he saw me changing clothes he would want to have sex then and there.

It didn't matter what my mood was or how I felt. He had to have sex even when I was sick, or tired, and once when we went to the beach and I was burned so severely by the sun I couldn't stand to be touched. It didn't matter to him. No matter how many times, no matter what I did, I could not satisfy him; he was insatiable. So I quit trying. I felt completely unloved and as though my only function was to provide him with sex. I stopped talking to him about it, and I stopped enjoying sex with him. It was simply something I did to be allowed to get up or to go the sleep.

At one point during this time I attempted suicide by taking a bottle of tranquilizers. Of course, they didn't hurt me a bit, they just made me oversleep, but I hadn't realized they were harmless. When Bill found out about it, he just assumed it was an attention-getting device. I told my OB-GYN about it, and he said that he would never have given me anything that I could hurt myself with, because he knew I was depressed. He suggested therapy, but I was not willing to attempt it. I was afraid of therapy. I was afraid that it would somehow fundamentally change who I was. I refused to try. It sobered me up some, because I didn't want to die, I only wanted to stop feeling so miserable. And, of course, within a few months I was feeling on top of the world again.

By 1970, three years into our marriage, I was having an affair with an attorney I met through Child Welfare. He was married also, and it only lasted a year. He took me to a downtown bar where professional men, attorneys and newspaper men hung out, and after the breakup, I went back there alone. Soon I was a full-fledged "bar slut," sleeping with every man who frequented the bar. There were so many I can't remember all their names. I'm certain the men thought little of me, but I was convinced I was looking for love. Looking back on it, I wonder that I had the nerve to keep showing my face there. One night I was introduced to Bob, who was a radio newsman. There was an instant connection the minute we saw each other and by February of 1971 we were having an affair. Bob was also married, and we saw each other once or twice a week, usually at a "hot sheet" motel, where we paid a couple of dollars for a couple of hours. Again, I didn't think of how cheap and sleazy this made me, just that I was being "loved" by someone.

I had earned my teaching certificate, but hadn't been able to get a teaching job. Those in the know about those things told me that the school districts had to pay an extra one thousand dollars to teachers with Masters' degrees, and they preferred not to do that, as long as they could get teachers with Bachelors' degrees. I was able to get some part-time teaching at Junior Colleges, and worked temporary jobs. Though I made casseroles on the weekend so he could just warm up his dinner while I taught in the evenings, Bill complained that I made him "cook" and once, when I burned myself preparing something, he refused to do the dishes for me. He said dishwashing was "women's work." I wasn't getting a lot of support at home.

Bill found a summer job in Winston-Salem, North Carolina and left on a several-week assignment. Meanwhile, I stayed home and in early 1973 landed a job as a social worker with the Dallas Police Department. By the time Bill returned, I was in love with Bob and torn. I now know that if I felt that strongly about Bob I should have left Bill and ended the marriage. But I had been raised with the idea that one does not end a marriage, and I simply did not know how. Besides, Bob was married and he didn't intend to leave his wife, either.

Bill went back to teaching math and I worked with prisoners in the city jail and with people in the community referred by police officers. Working with cops was interesting, and I learned a whole new culture. Still, I had my bad-judgment moments even as I had my satisfying ones. Luckily, I had the best boss at the police department I ever had in my working career, and he overlooked human frailty and always encouraged a person to do their best. It made you not want to let him down.

Jackie had been having trouble with her daughter, Terrie, with drugs and mental illness. She had committed her twice to a private mental health facility. Suddenly, there was a warrant out for Terrie's arrest and she couldn't go home because the police were watching her house. Jackie told her she had a choice; she could either go to jail or back to the healthcare facility. Jackie called me and asked me to pick Terrie up and take her to the mental hospital. So there I was, an employee of the police department taking a wanted person to a hospital instead of turning her in. I felt a little bad, but my first loyalty was to Jackie. Months later, I told my boss about it. He laughed, and said, "For goodness sake, don't worry -- I would have done the same thing." A truly good cop.

The worst thing I ever did and the most reckless was to purloin papers off this boss' desk regarding a project that Bob was pitching to the police department. He wanted to know how the department had reacted to his pitch, so I "borrowed" their report, copied it, and mailed it to him. Again, something only a manic person would risk. And something I have felt guilty about for years. But it seemed like a good idea at the time.

Partially driven to it by me, I'm sure, Bill had an affair with a co-worker. I couldn't be too angry with him, considering, but what upset me was the way he flaunted it. It hurts your pride when everyone knows about it, and he made sure that everyone, including me, knew all about it. I had managed to carry on like a Siamese cat in heat without rubbing his face in it.

After this, we decided to go to a marriage counselor, but for some reason, Bill insisted on going to the one recommended by his girlfriend, a man who was an ex-Baptist minister. I had a bad feeling about that, but had to go along with it. I had hopes for marriage counseling, too.

The counselor concluded that the problems in the marriage were caused by me. My problem was frigidity. I just needed to have more sex. Marriage counseling did not work out well for me.

No changes came about because of the affair or the counseling. Our marriage stayed in the same groove, with me resenting my role and carrying on an affair with Bob, and with others when Bob disappointed, and Bill still demanding sex and still not understanding how I felt. Something needed to happen to get us off dead center.

CHAPTER 17: And There is Fire In Every Single Heart

I was in a hospital bed, feeling woozy, recovering from a biopsy that was negative when Bill announced to me, excitedly, that he had gotten his dream job. I was happy in my job with the Police Department, but knew there was no chance for advancement there. I had been recruited to be a female police officer, since they were in dire need to meet their affirmative action goals, but in my heart I knew I did not have the cool-headed judgment for the job, even though I would have loved to have tried. I just knew I couldn't do it. A bad-judgment call for a police officer can be really bad. I didn't know I was bipolar at the time, I just knew I made a lot of mistakes that I couldn't seem to avoid and didn't have a lot of control. I knew a policeman had to have both good judgment and good control.

Bill's job was at the Jet Propulsion Lab in Pasedena, California, working as a electronic communications specialist in the space program. He had almost finished his Masters' Degree, and they would facilitate his obtaining his degree. I was not pleased at the idea of leaving my friends, especially Jackie, and moving to a strange place. I was especially not happy when I learned that he would serve his apprenticeship at Barstow, where the big communications satellite was located.

I thought long and seriously about simply not going with him. It would be the end of our marriage, and that might have been a good thing. But, again, I had been taught to stick with my marriage no matter what, so decided that maybe that was what our marriage needed -- a new start in a new place. We sold the house and set off. Bob and I broke up, both assuming that we would never see each other again.

83

Barstow was worse than I had expected.   Bill wanted to buy me a horse, something I had always wanted, but I couldn't imagine having a horse in such an awful climate.   In the summer the temperature often started out at 50 degrees in the morning and topped out at 125 in the afternoon.   It was both unpleasant and dangerous.   And, there were no trees.   That upset me more than I ever would have thought.   I just couldn't get used to a treeless desert.   In winter, the wind blew constantly and it was miserably cold.   Also, the first thing that happened was that our cat disappeared, and we weren't able to track her down for five weeks.   I was devastated at her loss, making me more homesick and sorrier that I had moved.

As for finding a job, Barstow was mostly a stopping-off place between Los Angeles and Las Vegas.   It was a town of motels and restaurants.   I tried for a teaching job, but was told that I couldn't teach there because I would "have to teach blacks." (What did they think we did in Texas -- keep them in concentration camps?)   The closest social work job I could find was in San Bernadino, which was sixty-five miles away.   When I suggested to Bill that I get a room there and come home on weekends, he pitched a fit and insisted that I get a job where I could be home every night.   He also insisted that I was lazy and had never contributed anything in our marriage when I couldn't find a job.

I settled into being a housewife for the first time in my life and of course fell into a deep depression.   I was miserable, felt I was in a deep hole that I couldn't get out of, and wanted to die.   I had no friends, no function. I spent most of my time reading and did little else.   Bill introduced me to one couple, but I had little in common with them.   We fought.   At one point he hauled off and hit me, hard, the only time he did that in our marriage.   It scared me badly, because I lost the hearing in one ear. I went to a doctor, who pretended along with me that I hadn't been abused.   He told me that my eardrum had been ruptured and would probably heal by itself, which it eventually did.   Of course, I should have just left, but didn't.

Bill accused me of being uninterested in his job.   The truth was that I had not a clue what he did all day.   I just knew that he tracked space capsules and men in space.   I honestly have no idea how a person goes about doing that, and if he tried to explain, my eyes would glaze over. Too much math.

For fun, we did a little prospecting of semi-precious gems and some rock-polishing, but that takes up only so much time. After a while, I developed an allergy to the slurry used to polish the rocks and had to give that up. I spent a great deal of my time watching the Watergate Hearings, which certainly did nothing to improve my mood. I was horrified at what Nixon's government had done, and amazed that it took so long to remove him from power. I was glued to the television for weeks, thinking that I was watching history being made.

And to tell the truth, I missed Bob. I didn't contact him, but I missed him. I felt so alone without friends or a job. Bill kept telling me that he was all I needed, that I shouldn't need anyone else. But I had always been gregarious, and needed the company of others. My depression and desperation grew.

Bill was supposed to serve two years in Barstow before he was transferred to Pasedena, but told his bosses that I was likely to commit suicide before then. He could see my desperation, and it gave him a good excuse to move to the city. They agreed to transfer him after only one year. I hoped things would improve once I got to the city.

CHAPTER 18: THERE ARE MONSTERS

We found the greatest house in Altadena, just north of Pasadena. We used my retirement fom the Dallas Police department for the down payment. It had four bedrooms and two baths, and fit our budget. It was just a few miles from the Jet Propulsion Lab, and, with time, I was sure I could find a job. First, I checked out law schools nearby since we had made the deal that after he got his Masters', it would be my turn for school, but he simply stated that he was not going to spend money on law school. Period. That deal was broken.

While I looked for work, I enrolled in a paralegal course at UCLA just to have something to do. I met a good ol' girl from Houston there, and she became a good friend. She had marital problems of her own, but introduced me to her friends and took me places with her. Mary was the best thing that happened to me in Los Angeles.

I learned my way around town as I looked for work, but found, to my great distress, that many still harbored a prejudice against Okies at that time. Some told me that I would have to prove that I was "stable" by living in the area for two years, others broke off the interview as soon as I clarified that the OU I attended was not Ohio University but Oklahoma.

Even with trees and grass and more reasonable weather, my mood did not improve. I stayed horribly depressed, wanting a job to materialize immediately. Our ninth wedding anniversary came around; I gave Bill some small, thoughtful gifts. His response was; "I don't think of us like that anymore." I received no gifts from him. When I would talk of leaving, though, he would beg me to stay. The messages from him were definitely mixed, and things were coming to a head. I wanted out, but had no way to leave. At least I thought so. Sometimes it's the little things that finally tip the balance.

Bill was a smoker when I met him. I had never smoked and did not like the smell of cigarette smoke, but I could not convince him to quit, even though he was not addicted. After living with him a couple of years, I started to smoke. And was immediately and irrevocably hooked. When his father died of lung cancer, he quit and demanded that I quit also. It was difficult for me, and I did not want to quit. I was having a lot of trouble with trying to quit smoking. Since he had just laid them down, he expected me to do so, also.

Then, I went to a job interview for clerical work as a temporary. I was told at the agency that I would never get a job in the Los Angeles area until I had speech therapy for my Texas accent. That night Bill showed me a picture in "Penthouse" and asked me to shave my "bush" like the girl's in the photo. That was simply the last straw on an overloaded camel's back.

The next morning I packed and asked him to drive me to the airport. I flew to Dallas and smoked a pack of cigarettes on the plane.

CHAPTER 19: THERE ARE ANGELS

I showed up on Jackie's doorstep with a suitcase and nothing else. She welcomed me and told me she was glad that I had finally made a move. All she had to offer me was half her king-size bed, but she did that gladly. All I knew at that point was that I had to get away and was not sure what my plans were. I knew that I could not stay in Dallas -- that I was much too in love in Bob to stay in town, single, while he was married. I had vague plans to move to Norman or Austin, both college towns where I thought I could get a job and be happy.

But of course, after staying up and talking with Jackie all night, at 8 a.m. I was on the phone to Bob's workplace to tell him I was in town. And came close to fainting, literally falling against the wall, when the first thing he said was, "Guess what? Sheila left me." We made plans to see each other, but now my situation was even more confused.

I spent the next six weeks trying to decide what to do. I just knew, even though I was depressed, that a huge load had been lifted off my shoulders. I felt free and ready to start a new life, but scared by my lack of a job. I had nowhere to live and no money. I felt so guilty about leaving even though Bill didn't want me to that I didn't want to ask him for money. At the same time, I didn't see how I could go back to that oppressive situation again, and I didn't see how I could live without money or a job.

I went home to Oklahoma City for Thanksgiving, and my parents told me that my Christmas presents had been mailed to Altadena. They said that I could have them when I returned to my senses and went home "where I belonged." I was not surprised by their lack of support, but I could have used some sympathy and understanding. Instead I was coldly told to return to my husband. It never occurred to them that I had reason to leave.   My place was with my husband and my mother had certainly modeled the correct behavior for me.

I worked some temporary jobs and got up enough money to rent a small apartment in the same neighborhood I had lived in before in Dallas.   I spent New Year's 1975 in my new place, all by myself.   I knew I would need a steady source of income to keep it up.   Also, I would need my car for serious job hunting.   I finally worked up the courage to fly back to Los Angeles, but was completely surprised by Bill's attitude.   He seemed to think that I had come back for good.   I tried to talk about the situation, but he wanted me to stay.

I was going to be making the long drive to Texas by myself, so wanted a pistol to take with me.   This necessitated a five-day wait.   Bill worked on me the whole time to change my mind.   The night before I left, I lay awake all night, trying to decide.   I cried all night, too.   It was a scary and a hard decision.   I felt guilty for wanting to end the marriage when he said he didn't, even though his actions told me differently. He wanted me to go to a marriage counselor and I agreed, but I knew that all I wanted the counselor to do was to explain to him that the marriage was over.   It seemed expensive and useless -- I could tell him that myself.   Finally, I realized that I couldn't stay.   I told him that I was leaving, he cried, and driving away was the most difficult thing I ever did.   But I was compelled to.

About the gun: my work with the Dallas Police Department had made me more aware that I could be the victim of a crime.   I had always been afraid to have a gun in the house because of my suicidal moods, but I had also learned from stories told by patrolmen friends that com- mitting suicide with a .22 caliber pistol was not a smart move, since it didn't always have the desired results.   It often did not end in death. Some people who tried it were left brain-damaged, others, maimed for life.   I felt that I could own a small gun without fear that I would turn it on myself because I didn't want to end up a vegetable.   I had one from then on as a single woman, but did not have it at hand when I had a break-in at 4 a.m. shortly after I left Bill.   I learned my lesson then, and always have it handy now.   Luckily the guy who broke in was looking for booty and was not a rapist or a murderer, but he scared me almost to death.

Finally, we agreed that Bill would pay my rent until I got a job. He also told me to stay in nice motels and take my time on the drive because he wanted me to be safe. He said he would pay for the motels, the meals, and the gas for the trip. Shortly after I got home, I received a large envelope from him. Receipts for expenses from my trip. I hadn't spent much money, only a hundred dollars for the whole thing, but he now told me now that he wouldn't pay and that I had to pay for it. It made me so mad I didn't argue; I just paid for it. That's what guilt will do -- the only settlement I got for the whole marriage was the rent he paid.

Over the next few weeks, I would waver and call to talk to him, but, to my surprise, when I called him after about a month, I discovered he had moved another woman into the house. After that, he was sure that I had made the right decision, but then he started telling me that I would never get any more money from him, that he would make sure I wouldn't get a penny. He said he would quit his job, disappear, let the house go, all so I couldn't get a penny from him. He would practically rave about it, and I felt so guilty and so ready to get out of the marriage that I agreed. So for those years of getting him through school, of living in poverty, and the later years, in misery, I got nothing. Later, when I talked to my psychiatrist about my marriage, she told me she thought Bill had bipolar disorder. That gave me a lot to think about. I had never suspected it because he was so good at hiding his feelings. But it would explain a lot.

CHAPTER 20: I'm Nobody's Promise

I continued to work temporary jobs; I knew my way around Dallas well and no one ever complained about my accent. It was enough to buy gas and pay for food. Bill continued to pay for my rent. I saw Bob pretty regularly, but he never took me out. He just came to my apartment. It also became obvious that he was seeing other women regularly. I had hoped that we would become a couple after we both left our spouses, but that did not happen. He was really enjoying his freedom.

Very soon after I moved to back Dallas, my love for him turned to obsession. I stalked him, but he didn't know. I would hang around his apartment, hidden, and watch him. I soon saw him with other women, and it bothered me a great deal. I was depressed over the failure of my marriage, and over the what I saw as the failure of my relationship. At least I knew I had not left my husband for him, but for myself. If I thought I had left my marriage for a relationship with Bob, I would have felt completely let down and like a failure.

For the first time, I felt that I needed help with my problems. I couldn't afford a private therapist, so I went to Dallas County Mental Health, which charged on a sliding scale. They saw me on a weekly basis, and immediately diagnosed me as depressed. My sessions consisted of one-on-one counseling with the therapist explaining to me that I was an attractive, intelligent woman who had a lot to offer and that I shouldn't be depressed. "You should just get over this depression. It is serving no purpose for you." I asked him over and over how I was to do that and he said that I should just not be depressed. "What you need to do is just start feeling better." After about four meetings I couldn't take any more of this and stopped going to counseling.

This was actually a negative experience for me, for it convinced me that counseling and therapy offered nothing to me and it would be years before I would try again. I could not see that I had been offered any help. Bob had predicted to me that I would not receive any help from counseling, and he was right. For many years afterward, when it was suggested that I get help, for example, from my doctor, I shrugged it off, because I couldn't bear to be preached to about how I shouldn't be depressed and I should simply get over it. It caused me to lose years that might have been productive if I had sought psychiatric help sooner.

In January 1976, Jackie helped me to get another job with the state welfare department. This time I would be certifying people for food stamps. I had a wonderful boss, Ron, who trained me well and I was to remain in this position for seven years. With this, Bill discontinued his rent payments to me and I was finally on my own. This was a great feeling. In December of 1976, I obtained a "no-fault" divorce, with a division of property that awarded me my car, my cat, my clothes, and my personal possessions. Bill kept the house and other household furnishings. It was good to have it over with. Later, I did receive a settlement of $3,500. It was little for what I had contributed to the marriage, but I was just so happy to have it over with that it was years before I realized how much I had given up, and that I had been entitled to more.

Ron, my boss, and I remained friends for years. When I told him I had been diagnosed with bipolar disorder, he said, "That's impossible." I said, "Why is it impossible?" He answered, "Because no one as intelligent as you are could be mentally ill." But it has nothing to do with intelligence. Bipolar disorder does not discriminate.

I made a good friend, Barbara, who started out as a worker with me and later became a supervisor. She remains my friend to this day, even through my mood changes and some of the difficulties I put her through on the job. The job was difficult due to the sheer amount of work that was expected and the fact that the Federal government set the standards for our work and the state paid the bills. Trying to serve both masters kept us between the devil and the deep blue sea. For three years, I did new application home visits, which meant I did seven home visits in a day, in the heat and cold, looking for addresses and trying to verify facts about people's living conditions all over southern Dallas. It was draining work. The other four years I worked in the office, seeing nine clients a day. The human misery piled high and got to me after a while, though the senior citizens were often pleasant and even fun to work with.

There was fraud to look out for and sheer human cussedness to deal with, clients who were mentally ill, and frustrating bureaucratic rules that often stymied us. It was a difficult job, and I worked it for seven years.

During this time, I "dated" Bob. A date consisted of him bringing over take-out food or me cooking. He usually called at 2 a.m., when the bars closed. He never, during the ten years I saw him, took me out. He never said, "I love you." We stayed in, watched TV or read, and had sex. The sex, though, was great. We never lost any of that. We always had this great yearning for each other. He once said, "You know, you were a one-night stand that went bad." He cracked me up with his humor and he was always fun and exciting.

As for me, I was completely obsessed with him. I never wanted to date anyone else, and lived for his phone calls. After a couple of years, I began to notice a pattern and kept track of his visits. I usually saw him once, twice, or three times a week for about six weeks, and then for about three weeks I didn't hear from him at all. The pattern stayed true, but I couldn't figure out why. He changed jobs often, and when he was between jobs he lived with me. Of course, I was happy to let him do so.

He had other habits that completely confused me. Some mornings he would get up and take an upper. Other mornings he would swing his feet out of bed and smoke a joint. I could not predict which it would be and I never understood how he chose his drug.

It was years later that I realized that he, too, was manic-depressive and was doing what so many of us do -- self-medicating in an effort to make ourselves feel better. It was during my time with him that I started smoking marijuana to help me sleep. It is difficult to sleep both during manic and depressive phases and I found it a great help in getting to sleep. I often woke up early in the morning, but at least I was able to get some sleep. During my time with him, there were weeks when I was upset over our relationship and did not eat or sleep for as long as a week. Many times I paced the floor all night, only to go to work with no sleep. I think that the pattern of his coming and going exemplified his manic and depressive phases -- he saw me during his down times and pursued other women when he was up. This is only a theory, not a diagnosis; but it makes sense to me now, though it didn't at the time.

It was simply not surprising that we couldn't maintain a normal relationship. After several years, and after him telling me that "I will never find anyone better for me than you" that I began to relax and to believe that he would not leave me for another. I simply ignored the other women and took what I could get. I do not believe that I would put up with such a relationship except that my father had shown me that men do not love and care for women, and I was used to such an attitude from men. And, I was obsessed with him.

We broke up a couple of times, but couldn't make it stick. Once I went five months without hearing from him, but knew the minute the phone rang on a Friday night that it was Bob. He said, "Can I come home?" and I said, "Of course." That's how simple it was for us. Another time, we had not spoken for three months after I caught him dating my 18 year-old neighbor when I dropped in on him at his apartment and we fell into each other's arms. To give an example of how things went with us, after we crawled out of bed, he explained that since it was Mother's Day I would have to leave because his mother was in town and he had a date with her for dinner that night. I happily went home, only to exit my apartment a couple of hours later to see him picking up my neighbor for a date. He called the next day to make up. I did, with the proviso that he never mix up our apartment doors again. He promised, but of course did not keep that promise.

We knew each other and understood each other and I could not conceive of ever living without him, though he had never made any kind of commitment. Five years went by like this.

CHAPTER 21:
AND I'M NOBODY'S CHORE

In 1980, Jackie, my best friend, the one who had always been there for me, the person who had taken me in when I had no place to go, told me she had terminal cancer. They found it too late for surgery, and she didn't want to undergo chemotherapy for just the few months it would give her after she discovered how sick it made her. All I could do for her was help her get food stamps when she was finally unable to work and be there for her at the end. For her, dying with dignity meant "leaving 'em laughing." I remember the last Saturday night I was with her with absolute clarity. Only her roommate, Linda, and I were there; no one else was allowed to see her looking like that. Her family would arrive later when there was no time left. This was my time with her.

For two hours she kept us in stitches. ("Well, at least I don't have to deal with the trauma of turning forty. I always wanted to weigh 120 pounds and look at me now!") Linda and I knew we'd better laugh with her this last time; she would not tolerate sadness. I couldn't believe she was so close to death. Her voice, her jokes, her intelligence, were all the same. It was only her looks that were altered. Finally, when I couldn't hang on anymore, I hugged her one last time, then stumbled outside to the lawn to weep in the dark. Linda followed me out, not to comfort me, but because she couldn't hold back the tears any longer, either. Jackie died early Wednesday morning.

Jackie's funeral was scheduled for Friday. I had to work that day, but would take off early. I saw Bob Thursday; he was in a strange mood. He had just come back into town after working in Indianapolis. He told me that he thought it was time we became a "real couple" and officially move in together. Of course I agreed with him, but didn't push for a timetable or details. I was upset over Jackie's death and figured there was plenty of time to work things out. Bob told me that he had left some things in Indianapolis, which struck me as rather strange, and that he would pick them up and return Monday, when we could decide what to do. I agreed, rather absentmindedly, I will admit, and Friday morning I said good-bye for the weekend.

I got through the funeral, mostly because I thought I was going to get what I had dearly wanted for years -- a real relationship with Bob. Come Monday, though, he didn't return. I wasn't concerned until the weekend when he still wasn't back. As time went by and he still didn't show up, I became more and more depressed. I still waited, because I knew he would come, but something in the back of my head asked me "what if this is the time he doesn't return?"

By the end of the year, even though I am five feet, five inches tall, I weighed in at 98 pounds. I couldn't sleep, couldn't eat, and stayed by the phone every night and weekend.

Even the most routine tasks of life seemed impossible, every problem seemed insurmountable. I simply could not accept the fact that he had really left me for good. I left work every day and cried all the way home, weeping into the evening while I waited to hear from him. I blew up at the slightest thing, and work was becoming impossible. Months went by, then years. After two years, I still waited, but knew he wasn't coming back. I loved him just as much, and felt there must be something wrong with me that he didn't feel the need to let me know his plans. Every day that passed, I became more depressed. And obsessed. I don't know how my friends put up with me during this period. I couldn't think of anything but Bob. And I did little except wait by the phone. In fact, I became isolated.

I tried to date others, but simply couldn't sustain even the most superficial of relationships because all I wanted was Bob. However, one experience exemplifies what I think is a common experience. People with mood disorders attract others with mood disorders. I was sitting in a club with a friend when a good-looking guy walked in. I turned to her and said, "Look at him! I wish he would sit over here!" I lost sight of him in the crowd, but a few minutes later, when I turned around, he was sitting next to me. We started talking, and dated for a while, but with both of us extremely depressed, it was doomed from the start. I don't know how we recognize each other, but I am convinced we know and are attracted to those who are like us and will understand us.

I became less and less functional, less and less able to do my job and to handle everyday life. I had been trying to get a promotion or to transfer laterally at work because I was simply so tired of doing the same job day after day. I got the distinct impression that I was getting nowhere because I was not black; later, my supervisor confirmed that there was a big push on to promote blacks during the time I was trying to change jobs. I know it was frustrating to me to apply over and over and never get another job. Possibly it had gotten around that I was difficult, also. I'm not sure that I would have held onto my job for so long if my boss hadn't been Barbara, my friend. Finally, feeling that I was never going to succeed, I simply quit my job.

CHAPTER 22: AND I AIN'T GOT NOBODY TO LIVE FOR

I was scared to death. One day I was just lying in bed, doing nothing, when I suddenly felt that someone had hit me in the back with a sledgehammer. I was in incredible pain. I went to the doctor, and he told me my back pain was caused by pure stress. I had made the decision to take a teaching job with a small private school, but the pay was so little I had to depend on my retirement from the state to make ends meet. The back pain went away once I started teaching, but it was a sign of the fear and depression. I taught five subjects, so the work was hard, but different from what I had been doing. I got along well with most of the students, many of whom came from troubled backgrounds. My job was not only to teach them, but to form a warm, advisory relationship with them to help them in their personal lives as well. I was able to succed at this, and felt good about the work I was accomplishing.

However, my depression did not lift and I could not continue working there because I wasn't making enough money to support myself. Each month I had to dip into my savings just to pay my basic expenses. I had to make some kind of decision about my life. I kept returning to how safe and happy I felt when I was in college in Norman, and decided I would return to a simpler place to live. I thought that getting out of the big city and returning to a simpler place (and time?) would solve my problems. When school let out, I would move to Norman and get a job at the University. I went so far as to check with an old boyfriend from college, Ron, who still lived in Norman, as to job prospects. (He was the guy I dated while he waited to go into the Navy so many years before.) He told me that the University had a job freeze on and that it would be a bad time to count on a job there, but my mind was made up and I wasn't going to be deterred by reality.

At the end of the school year in 1983, I bade my students good-bye at graduation, gave up the apartment I had lived in since I left Bill, packed up my possessions, and left for Norman. I thought I was making a new start and that my life would improve immeasurably. The only pang was that Bob would no longer be able to find me; but I really thought that he wouldn't be looking for me by this time, anyway. We both had such common names that once I moved he would not be able to locate me or me him. He'd been gone two years.

I found a little apartment near campus, got a University library card, and started looking for work. After I had looked for a while, I realized that Ron had steered me straight -- there simply wasn't any work to be had. Naturally, the students had just about all the off-campus work sewed up, so I tried to enroll and that's when I found out that they would use last year's income to determine my financial help. I was not eligible for much help since I worked full time the year before. I had little money and that put my plan to enroll out of sight. I was stuck with no way to go to school and no job. So while I was happy to be back in Norman, I had placed myself in a dead end. I didn't know what to do, so I did nothing. My last option hadn't paid off.

One day I was running an errand and found myself driving the car as if I were furious, driving too fast and steering like a maniac. "Weird," I thought, "I don't feel angry, I don't feel anything at all." When I got home, I decided I needed help. Without thinking any more about it, I picked up the phone book and make an appointment with the community mental health center. I didn't really make a decision to seek mental health therapy, it just seemed like the only thing to do. I had already given away my stash of marijuana, because it was having no effect on me at all. Nothing. I wasn't sleeping, I was having trouble eating, and now this. I knew nothing about me was normal. I had reached a dead end.

The day of my appointment, I showed up early because I was used to going places in Dallas, where you had to leave extra time in case of traffic tie-ups or if you got lost, or whatever. The doctor laughed at me and said he understood, because he had done his internship in Dallas and did the same thing when he first came to Norman. His name was

Gary Kula, and he was understanding and easy to talk to. After only a few minutes he put me at ease and got me to tell my story.

He summed it up easily for me. He told me that I was not angry, but frightened, panicked. He said that I had given myself one last chance to make it, and had decided that if I didn't succeed, I would have to kill myself. He said that I hadn't necessarily consciously told myself that, but that had been my decision when I moved to Norman. He told me that I was extremely depressed and that he would prescribe an antidepressant and have me follow-up with visits to a social worker with weekly visits with him. I went away feeling better, but still confused about what would happen. I know that when I put those antidepressants in the medicine cabinet, I felt a stab of fear each time I walked into the bathroom because he had told me that an overdose would be fatal. I was not certain I could be trusted with them.

I had told Dr. Kula that I wasn't sleeping, just as I had told so many doctors before. He said, "I know you aren't, but with these pills you will sleep. Trust me." The first day I took them I slept for twenty-four hours. That was wonderful, just to sleep. Then I took my OU library card and tackled the library. I read everything about depression that I could find, and caught myself up on medications and the new theories about brain chemistry. I read for days, learning everything I could. I wanted to know what I was taking and what the effect should be. Back then, the drugs took ten days to two weeks to take effect, and it was that long before I noticed a difference. Meanwhile, I kept my appointments with the social worker and the doctor, and it was great to be able to talk to people who didn't talk down to me or to underestimate just how awful I felt. After about a week and a half, I looked up some of my new friends in Norman and we went to a movie. It was the first time in months I had felt like doing anything.

One morning I woke up shaking and with a stomach ache. Dr. Kula had told me to write things down that were bothering me so I started to write, remembering something from my childhood that up until now, I had no explanation for. One of the kinds of depression I had read about in my research was *anaclitic depression*, a depression of infants that led to failure to thrive. I had learned about failure to thrive when

I worked at Child Welfare, but now something rusty had clicked in my brain and I was upset.

When my baby sister was about a year old, she had stopped putting on weight and had slowly lost weight. She had been unable to use the nutrients in her food, and finally, had been fed only bananas. We had banana custard and banana pudding until even today I cannot look a banana in the face. She lost weight steadily despite all the doctor's tests and remedies. He could not find anything wrong with her. Finally, when she was almost a skeleton, she was admitted to the hospital for a full work-up. Again, they could find nothing wrong with her and she was discharged home to die.

My mother was beside herself. That night, while my father was at work, she bathed the baby in Lourdes water and had us all pray the rosary, begging for a miracle. At the time I was a bit nonplussed, because I was already into my atheist period and did not believe in miracles. My mother was certain, though, that Mary, the mother of Jesus, wouldn't let her baby die.

The next morning the baby ate normally for the first time in months. She ate, she retained and used her food, and she gained weight. She was perfectly normal. I still didn't believe in miracles, but obviously something had happened. I was confused, but simply didn't know what happened.

That day in Norman, it came to me that for some reason, perhaps because a fifth child was too much, or because my father was so disappointed that she again had a girl, my mother had become depressed and was unable to offer the child the warmth she needed. She became more depressed as the baby got sicker and sicker. However, when she became convinced that the child would become well after the Lourdes water and the prayers, her depression lifted and she was able to relate to the baby, bringing her out of the failure to thrive mode. It all made perfect sense, but the knowledge scared me. Had things been so bad at home and I just did not see it? True, I was only eight at the time, but I had no clue that we were living over the edge. That was the first time I realized that I had been surrounded and raised in serious mental illness. And that I had it too.

104

I had also found out that I could not live so close to my father. He kept showing up unannounced, trying to help me out and then getting angry; for example, he wanted to mow my grass once and I asked him not to because the landlord had just treated the lawn for fleas. He threw a tantrum and stormed off, vowing to never try to help me again. Then something else would happen, another tantrum would be thrown, and it was just like when I was a child.

The antidepressants did their work and I began to feel much better and much more confident in myself and my abilities. As a matter of fact, I began to feel very good. I saw the social worker and Dr. Kula exchange a significant look at one point as I raved about how wonderful I felt, but they didn't say anything at the time. I made plans to return to Dallas, feeling that I could handle anything. I knew I could find some kind of work in Dallas, and there wasn't any in Norman. Much as I loved the town, it was time to get back to my real life.

CHAPTER 23: NOBODY TO LIVE FOR

I returned to Dallas feeling like I could conquer the world in September 1983. I would continue my medication at the Dallas County Community mental health center. I had no job, but felt that I could get one without a problem. In fact I went back to work as a temporary right away to support myself.

My first visit back to the mental health center was eye-opening. Now they had a pharmacy window and there was no talk therapy. Unlike the bright, clean clinic in Oklahoma, this one was dirty and dingy, with clerks who treated patients as if they were less than human. The doctor I was assigned to informed me that I was bipolar and when I objected, showed me the letter Dr. Kula had sent, diagnosing me as such. I didn't know much about manic-depression but decided to go along with Dr. Kula's diagnosis, since I had been able to trust him so far.

The doctor continued me on antidepressants, which had the unfortunate side effect of making me feel thirsty all the time, and added lithium. Between the lithium and the antidepressants I began to gain weight -- a lot of it, which was a shock for me, since I had been so small for so long. I would eventually top out at 160 pounds. Lithium is the first drug of choice for bipolar disorder since it helps the majority of people with the disorder. However, bipolar disorder is an individual disease and individual react differently to medications. Sometimes a person will have to try several, frustratingly, before they find the right med or the right combination of meds for their particular disorder.

I then started to educate myself about bipolar disorder. I could find only one book about it in the library, and it didn't sound much like me. I didn't lose touch with reality, and I never went on spending sprees -- at least I didn't spend more than I could handle. Maybe I would buy four lipsticks when I only needed one, or buy things that I really didn't need, but I never put myself in debt. I just couldn't see it.

Eventually, though, as I thought about my history and how I had handled things all my life, I began to see bipolar disorder as a possibility. Perhaps I didn't fit all of the parameters of the disease, but I certainly had my ups and downs and I had made life difficult for myself throughout my history. I was willing to try the therapy to see if it would help.

For a time, I attended a bipolar support group, but I didn't stick with it. I wanted to stablize the disease with medication and live as though I didn't have it. I really thought that was possible and I didn't want to be thought of as "sick." I was sure I could order things so I could be "normal" and I didn't want to be lumped with sick people. I think this was a mistake and I would continue with the support group if I had it to do over again. The people in my group had "real" problems while I had it under control. I didn't need their help, and was especially upset when one girl whom I really liked got into a shoot-out with police and was sent to the hospital. I knew about "suicide by cop" and that scared me. No, I was sure I had nothing in common with these people.

I could see no improvement with the lithium. It was not what I needed. The doctor insisted that it was the drug that would help me. When I objected that I was not getting any help from it, he told me that I was "crazy" and couldn't know what was good for me. Only he, the doctor, was capable of making that judgment. Dallas County did not hire psychiatrists to work in the clinic, but retired medical doctors. They did not know medications like psychiatrists do, and if I had known what I was doing, I would have gone to a private psychiatrist (finding the money somehow) or moved to a different state. (Texas ranks 47th among the states in per capita mental health spending.)[4]

The time I wasted and the pain I felt were not worth it. Just staying in Oklahoma would have meant much better care. Perhaps I would have been getting the medication I needed without a waste of the next five years while I tried to obtain proper care in Dallas. However, there was the job problem. It was difficult; in an age of computers I could have done research about the best place to live.

Meanwhile, I was lonely. I wasn't dating and didn't want to go to bars to meet someone. Not only had I not had much luck that way, but I could no longer drink since I was taking medication. I felt well enough to make a decision that would change my life. I decided to join Mensa, which had become a nationwide organization since I had first heard of it in 1964. I remembered that my principal in high school had told my parents that I had scored in the top two percent of the population on my IQ test, so I knew I was eligible. I sent off for my high school IQ scores, and mailed them into the Mensa national office. It took a few weeks, but I was accepted for membership and directed to my local group in Dallas.

CHAPTER 24: I'm Nobody's Work

"Ralf Kittenbacher."
Alpha Photography

Excited, anxious, and determined, I drove to my first Mensa function in April, 1984. I was excited because I was going to meet new people, anxious about what they would think of me, and determined to meet a new boyfriend. I had been without a significant other since 1980, and I was tired of being alone. I remember saying out loud in the car on the way, "Well, Bob, if you are ever going to come back you'd better do it now, because I am going to find someone new to go out with tonight!"

The function was a New Member's Party, and I had a great time. There were over a hundred members of Mensa there and I met lots of new people, all of whom seemed pleasant. The evening went by in a blur with lots of great food and many people to talk with. I went home exhausted, happy, and with a date for the next weekend. I had a date with Tom, who turned out to be one of the kindest, gentlest, most loving persons I have ever met. He was exactly what I needed at this time in my life. He reminded me what it was like to really date someone, to actually go out and do things together.

And Mensa was exactly the organization I needed. Set up as a social meeting place for people with an IQ in the top two percent of the population, it accepted everyone on an equal basis and members were not too surprised if an individual turned out to be somewhat eccentric.

We all got along together and overlooked faults.

My relationship with Tom lasted only a year, but I believe that it was the only time I was truly loved for myself, with someone accepting me strictly as I am. It healed the cuts left by Bob and restored my self-confidence. The acceptance I found by Mensa members gave me somewhere to go and friends I could rely on. Later, when I found the proper medication and became stable, I was elected to local office in Mensa three times. Meanwhile, while I was searching for treatment, I had support and people who cared about me.

There was a party to attend every weekend and people to talk with. As long as I dated Tom, I had a date. When we broke up, I felt confident to continue attending, and soon met another man. It gave me a social life and kept me from being so isolated and alone. I owe the organization and the local group -- North Texas Mensa -- a great deal of gratitude for making my life so much easier and, in my rougher times, perhaps, for saving my life.

And there were some rough times. Besides being on the wrong medication, I had to have a hysterectomy in 1985 because of fibroids that caused bleeding. Afterwards, my doctor insisted that I be maintained on hormone replacement therapy. From what was known and thought about it at the time, I was also eager to do so. However, after a few weeks, I began to suffer from periodic, debilitating migraine headaches. Remembering that the only other migraine I had ever had was when I took my first course of birth control pills, I suspected that somehow the hormones were causing the headaches. The doctors said that was impossible.

Since it was thought at that time that hormone replacement therapy was really important for a woman's health, I kept trying to take the hormones and trying to find a way to stop the migraines, but received little help from physicians. The migraines made it difficult to hold down a job, and I was fired from a couple of temporary positions because of them. I also suffered in Mensa, because I would take on a volunteer job, only to have to bail because of headaches. I became an undependable person.

I was suffering excruciating pain that knocked me out for two days about every two weeks. My cholesterol level skyrocketed and my blood pressure was so high it was obscene. The doctor's response was to give me cholesterol-lowering and blood-pressure lowering medication for the symptoms, but not to try to find the cause. I was so frustrated and unhappy about the condition that after a year or so I simply stopped taking the hormones. Miraculously, the headaches stopped immediately, and my blood pressure dropped to normal. As a result of all this non-treatment, I developed a distrust of medical professionals then that has never completely dissipated.

Doctors are people, too, and some of them do not know how to deal with patients with mood disorder or mental illness. Anytime you find yourself dealing with a doctor or a healthcare professional who is prejudiced against someone with a mental illness, learn from my mistake and simply leave. Find a healthcare professional who is open with all of his or her patients and who is not afraid to deal with a person who has a mood disorder. One neurologist insisted that I was not having migraines, that I only thought that I was. He would say, "Well, you are mentally ill, you know." He refused to give me any pain medication because he was sure I was having delusions.

You will never get good treatment from a doctor, dentist, or other healthcare professional who is not open to treating you as an individual with your individual problems. If he or she has stereotyped ideas about mentally ill people, you will be placed in a box and never be treated properly. A doctor or dentist who is blinded by prejudice is not able to treat you and may make mistakes or miss something. This could result in serious problems for you, so if you find yourself in this situation ask to speak to a supervisor or leave and find another facility.

I have suffered for thirty-five years with kidney stones and have never had a problem with my urologists. I told two of them about my problems getting pain medication from other doctors, and both just shrugged and said, "People with bipolar disorder feel pain, too."

While I was home recuperating from my hysterectomy, I decided to go visit my current boyfriend because I was bored just sitting around by myself. Now I knew this was stupid, but I did it anyway. I was flying higher than I kite and I drove him nuts for several days. He knew I was manic-depressive, and he knew that it was the illness that was making me so out of control, but not even I was surprised when he subsequently broke up with me.

Even when I was fighting with my husband, or so manic I seemed to be flying, there was a part of me that dispassionately observed what was going on and knew it was crazy. But I couldn't stop my actions. I'd say to myself, "Self, this is nuts. You need to stop this," but I'd keep right on doing whatever crazy stuff I was doing. It takes more understanding than most people have to realize that the person cannot control his or her actions when they are manic or depressed. Not having control of your moods means not having control of your actions.

Meanwhile, I continued to try to convince the doctors at the Mental Health Clinic that lithium was not the drug for me. After my hysterectomy, due either to the reaction to the anesthetic or body chemistry changes, I became toxic on lithium. I was not able to even sign my name, my hands trembled so. I was so manic I drove myself crazy. And I had auditory hallucinations -- I kept hearing music inside my head. Now this will drive a person nuts. It was difficult to concentrate on anything with music going on all the time and going to sleep was really hard. It went on for days.

I didn't lose touch with reality. I knew the music was a hallucination and that I needed a medication adjustment to make it stop. Even now I don't know if it was caused by too much lithium or if it was a psychotic reaction, but I got to my doctor and explained something had to be done. He agreed the lithium was too much when he saw how I was shaking, but he diagnosed me as psychotic. He put me on Thorazine, a drug for highly psychotic patients, and on Haldol, a drug for flagrantly manic patients. The music finally stopped, which was a great relief. I have never had that particular symptom again. I have a tendency to believe that it had to do with an overdose of lithium, but, again, I don't really know.

Later, he dropped the Thorazine but added Navane, another drug for psychoses. He kept assuring me that if we kept adjusting the dosages of these drugs along with the lithium and antidepressant I was on, I would become stable. I didn't seem to feel better inside my head, and told him so. He told me just to have faith in him.

114

CHAPTER 25:
AND I'M NOBODY'S COMPANY

In the summer after I joined Mensa, I got a job with the Dallas Housing Authority, certifying applicants for Section 8 housing. I soon learned there were real problems with the job, for example, the supervisor broke all the integration rules by placing blacks with blacks and whites and whites, saying they would be "more comfortable" that way. I knew the mess would eventually hit the fan . There were other problems that would eventually surface, but I needed the job, so I kept a low profile and tried to look for another job as I worked. On the plus side, the Housing Authority was only a few blocks from my apartment.

My migraines and my difficulties with medication did not make things any easier, but I was able to hang in for two years. It was a fairly easy job, a great deal like certifying people for food stamps, but there were no emergencies and the workload was not so heavy.

After two years, I reported to my supervisor that one of my coworkers was accepting favors in return for moving people up the list for interviews. Shortly thereafter I was unceremoniously "laid off." I thought it was a pretty good time to leave, so didn't fight it. I'm pretty sure my difficulties in getting along with the other employees had a great deal to do with the lay-off , also. Mania, made permanent by taking antidepressants, does not have a salutary effect on one's ability to get along with others.

When my doctor at the mental health center went on vacation, I talked to another. This doctor asked me if I heard voices, saw things that weren't there, or generally lost touch with reality. I told him about the only time I had hallucinations, and he replied that the anti-psychotic drugs I was taking were doing me no good, and could be dangerous.

He told me in no uncertain terms to stop taking them, or risk tardive dsykinesia. Tardive dsykinesia is an illness caused by taking anti-psychotic drugs that causes involuntary movements of the face, head, and sometimes arms. I had seen patients with this problem and knew that if I suffered from it I would never work again. I immediately went off the anti-psychotic medications.

However, now I was without a job. And now, I was only on antidepressants. I had stopped the migraines by simply not taking hormones. I went off them against medical advice, but found that the migraines stopped immediately and, despite what the doctors said about the quality of my life, knew that I would eventually commit suicide if forced to live with migraines much longer. I was never given any pain medication for the migraines, and the pain was truly awful.

I told my regular doctor that I had gone off anti-psychotic medications when I next saw him because I feared not working anymore, and his reply, "'Well, you'll probably never work again, anyway" caused me to demand a change in doctors. I refused further anti-psychotic medication and became known as a "non-compliant" patient. This label means that a patient refuses therapy and, therefore, is not worth working with. I did not receive any help or any effort from a doctor after this. From then on, I just received a basic dosage of antidepressants, which had the effect of keeping me manic all the time. I did not realize that I was constantly manic, but I did know that I wasn't depressed, so I continued to take them.

I was able to land a teaching position with a couple of sections of American history in a junior college, which barely kept body and soul together. I also picked up some temporary jobs, but my constant mania meant that my relationships were suffering and that my concentration and performance were not up to par. The administrators were not happy with me at the college and the temporary jobs became fewer and farther between.

In 1987 and 1988, it was all I could do to pay for rent and food. I was barely making it and I was scared all the time. It was during that time that I can also remember shoplifting. I stole some eye shadow that I wanted and couldn't afford from a grocery store where I was well known.   It was exceedingly stupid and just shows how reckless I had become.   I'll never know if I wasn't seen or if they just decided to let it go.   It wasn't like I needed the eye shadow -- it was something I wanted and couldn't afford on my meager budget, so I just took it.   I don't remember thinking about it or making a decision to steal it.   It was there. I wanted it. I took it.   I was so high that there was no guilt attached.   I took it without thinking about it or worrying about the consequences.   It was just another indication of how high I was and how poor my judgment was.

I had boyfriend after boyfriend during this time. My relationships never lasted for a long time, but I always had one.   However, to give you an example of the quality of them -- one of my relationships during this time was with Jerry.   He was one-sixteenth Cherokee Indian but insisted that he was a Native American and spent his time complaining about how the white man had stolen the Indians' land.   Since my grandmother was one of these white people, this had a tendency to make me uncomfortable.   Even though I was 42 years old, he monitored every thing I ate, insisting that I did not eat properly.   Finally, when we argued about anything, he drove me crazy by making up "facts" to bolster his side of the dispute.   Despite all these drawbacks, it took me months to toss him out.

My life was spinning out of control.   I had done some substitute teaching in public schools and was blown away by the way students treated their teachers.   I couldn't see myself teaching in the public school system, since I didn't believe I could manage the students without blowing up, and I already knew I couldn't make enough as a private school teacher.   I couldn't face social work again.   I was just completely burned out on that.   So, what was I to do? I was jobless, barely eking out a living, blowing all my relationships and high as a kite.   I figured it out -- I'd go back to school!

CHAPTER 26: EVERY TIME
I TURN AROUND

I had long wanted to try law school, but felt financially that was out. I couldn't afford three years of school, and shuddered at the thought of borrowing that much money. But I thought I could try paralegal school. The thought of going back to school and gaining new skills cheered me tremendously. I thought I would be making a new start in a new field and it would solve all my problems. If that sounds a bit simplistic and even manic, it was.

The first thing I did was check with the social worker at the mental health center to see if there were funds to help me go back to school. Without even looking at me, she casually said, over her shoulder, "No, there's no help for someone like you." Later, when I was talking to the manager of the center about how difficult it was to keep my medical appointments while going to school, she asked me why I hadn't secured the money to go to school from Texas Rehabilitation. I told her I had asked the social worker and been turned down.

That evening the social worker called me, and obviously covering her ass, asked me to recall that she had set up a meeting to discuss with me the possibility of funding school through Texas Rehab, but I had told her that I didn't want to attend the meeting. I told her that I remembered no such thing, and she told me that was what was documented in my record. (As if I would have turned down $5,000 in aid so casually). Later, she was named "Social Worker of the Year." I ran into this time after time. When you are "mentally ill," you are always wrong. If your medication is messed up, if you are screwed out of money, if your appointment is fouled up, if your check is lost, you are always the one at fault. Always, always, make sure that everything you do with an agency or doctor is thoroughly documented because they know this. They can always blame the crazy person for any mistake, and you have no defense.

I found the best paralegal school in Dallas and enrolled there, borrowing several thousand dollars to pay for the school and my living expenses while I attended. The school lasted some five months and was intensive. Some of the students had difficulty with the speed and depth with which we were expected to learn, but I found it not as difficult as grad school.

During class I managed to drive everyone crazy. I was manic, always fidgeting and chewing on ice, asking the teacher endless questions and making comments. I couldn't help myself. I didn't make any friends and did not know how disliked I was until I ran into a fellow student downtown and she cut me dead. I did not do as well in school as I should have, but I managed to graduate in December of 1988. I had high hopes of finding a job. However, I had heard rumors in school that lawyers liked young paralegals and did not care to work with older ones. That did not bode well.

I started off with temporary jobs. They were more lucrative than most temporary jobs, but more demanding. If you did not please the bosses in every way, you were fired. I lost a few, but managed to make enough money to keep me going for a few months. However, by the summer I was broke and I knew I was out of control. I was losing too many jobs, was getting a bad reputation in the legal field, and I was scared. Nothing was going right. I had the same feeling I had back in Norman seven years before. I needed help. I just had to find a place where I could get the help I needed. I had reached a dead end at the mental health center and I was desperate.

Somehow I had the idea that private mental hospitals had to have a bed or beds for public patients. I don't know where I got that idea, but I decided to try to find a place for myself. I didn't want to go to the state hospital because the minimum stay was six weeks and, judging from the care I had received from the mental health clinic, I was pretty sure it would be a complete waste of time.

So I sat down with the telephone book and started calling all the private mental hospitals in town. None of them knew what I was talking about. After ten or fifteen calls, I finally got so frustrated I told one of them, "Well, if I can't get any help, I guess I'll just have to kill myself!" (And I really felt that way. I had just about reached the end of my rope.) This scared her so much that she called the Dallas Police Department, and two patrolmen came to my home to see if I was about to off myself.

They were young, very Boy Scout, concerned about me, and a little shaky on the concept of mental illness. ("Now don't you be taking any of those pills -- they'll make you crazy!"). But they knew something that was a tremendous help to me -- they referred me to the Mood Disorders Clinic at Parkland Hospital. Parkland is a teaching hospital for the University of Texas Southwestern Medical School, so when you are in the hospital, and not attending the outpatient clinic, which is overloaded and understaffed, you get excellent care. I hadn't known about the clinic, and wouldn't have known how to get a referral, either. The cops called in the referral and, after making arrangements with my neighbors and good friends, Shirley and Karen, for my cats to be cared for, I was off to the hospital.

CHAPTER 27: I Always Seem to Find

I stood outside the locked doors of the Ninth Floor of Parkland Hospital perusing the papers I had to sign to be admitted. Never having been in a mental hospital before, I had no idea what to expect. The first thing I had to do was to sign myself in as a suspected crazy person. The papers surprised me -- I was signing myself in voluntarily, but when I wanted to leave, the doctors had three days to decide whether or not I would be allowed to do so. Hmmm, that was not what I was expecting. I thought that I could leave at any time. But desperate times call for desperate measures, so I signed the papers and was allowed in.

I was assigned to a room that looked more like a dorm room than a hospital room. I had a roommate, who I would meet later. My shampoo and conditioner were taken from me, along with other personal care products. I didn't like the look of that, either. I was not allowed to keep a mirror or any sharp objects.

When I saw the young residents and interns scurrying around the ward, I realized that I had done something I always had been advised not to do. I had checked myself into a teaching hospital at the end of June just before the new crop of interns and residents came on board. Well, it was too late for regrets now. I was going to be training doctors and it was all up to the luck of the draw. The nurses were all psychiatric nurses and were middle-aged. It looked like some of the staff knew what was going on.

Before joining the population, I was briefed on the rules. Smoking was allowed on this ward only, because it is so difficult for people with mood disorders to quit smoking. I was supposed to take part in all activities, to keep my room neat, and to ask permission to do just about anything. Again, since it was a teaching situation, I would be undergoing testing for just about everything -- and I would be cooperative. The doors to the ward were locked. We were checked on at night every quarter-hour. We were not to be in our rooms alone except to be in the bathroom. Since I am rather a loner, this was starting to sound difficult. But I wanted treatment, so of course I agreed.

I had a long interview in which I gave my medical history and described my long battle to get proper mental health care. I also gave a social history. I startled the nurse when I told her I had twenty-seven separate jobs in the past three years. Then I went through the same thing with my intern. After that, the day was nearly over, so I met my roommate and obtained my shampoo and conditioner so I could get ready for bed. I decided the shampoo thing was simply a control measure -- have you ever heard of suicide by shampoo?

All night long, the door would open and the nurse would flash a light around to make sure we weren't doing anything forbidden, like killing ourselves. It was distracting, but I would get used to it and learn to sleep right through the bed checks. The next morning, I went through the ordeal of obtaining a mirror so I could sit on the floor in the hall and put on my make-up. We had to do it in public so we couldn't break a mirror and hurt ourselves. However, if we wanted to shave our legs, or when the men shaved, we checked out a razor and shaved in private. It was all strange and somewhat absurd.

That day they started scheduling each of us for batteries of tests, more for the benefit of our doctors than for us. I met my resident that day. His name was Jim Shupe, and he listened patiently to my story of the many medications that I had taken, none of which had seemed to do any good for my manic-depression. Dr. Shupe was a man of few words and after my outpouring, he simply said, "Well, I guess we won't give you lithium." For the first time I felt that someone had heard me. He prescribed Tegretol, an anti-seizure medication, which I would start as soon as the other meds were out of my system. No one really knows why anti-seizure medications work with bipolar disorder, he explained, but for some reason they seem to work when lithium does not. I was hopeful for the first time that something positive would come out of the experience.

After this I met the other patients. There were something like sixteen of us -- mostly mood disorders, which are primarily depressed and bi-polar patients. But there was also a patient with obsessive-compulsive disorder, a young girl with schizoid personality disorder, a young boy with mild schizophrenia, and even a patient with multiple personality disorder. Between activities, which included art, exercise, and other time-killers, we learned each other's stories.

The young, good-looking kid, Tim, was getting out in a couple of days. I've never seen anyone so pleased. He told me that his father had thrown him out of the house for taking drugs, and he had moved in with a friend. His friend's mother asked him why he took drugs, and he explained that he was trying to shut up the voices in his head. She told him that he shouldn't have voices in his head and looked around to find him help. He was just eighteen, but old enough to sign himself into Parkland. With just a minimal dose of Haldol, the voices had gone away and he said he had found peace for the first time in years. He understood that he couldn't take street drugs anymore, and that he had to take Haldol from then on, but he was eager to get out of the hospital and get on with his life. His friend's mother had explained things to his parents, and he was going home.

Jean was obsessive-compulsive, and couldn't make her visions go away. They intruded on her life and made her nonfunctional. She was be-ing treated in a way to teach her to handle the visions so she could go back to work. She was being treated behaviorally, without medication, which I thought was a mistake, but it sure wasn't my call. If I had been her, I would have been raising hell.

The young girl was a "cutter," a person who cut herself compulsively with a razor blade. She didn't know why or how to stop it. I never learned her treatment, or how successful it was, since she stayed after I left. Her father, who was a prominent dentist, brought us all a gallon of pricey ice cream one day. After we each had a serving, we put the rest away for the next day. That night, one of the nurses' aides, (aides were not always the most professional people), ate all of the rest. When you are locked up, and ice cream is a big part of the day, that kind of injustice hurts. We were all angry the next day when we wanted our ice cream and found it gone.

The girl with multiple personality disorder stayed completely away from the rest of us, and seemed to be there just so the doctors could learn about her. She was always on suicide watch, and we learned nothing about her or her treatment.

I remember being allowed to stay up late, sitting in the hospital's windows watching the city's Fourth of July fireworks. It was probably the best view I ever had of the whole city's displays, but being locked up in the hospital didn't make me feel festive.

Some of the patients loved being in the hospital. They had no responsibilities, had their food provided for them, their lives scheduled for them, and made no decisions. I hated it. I hated having to ask for my own possessions, I hated being scheduled, and I purely hated being locked up. For example, a former patient who had been on the ward and missed the daily paper during his stay now paid for a subscription for us. Every day we read the newspaper, except for the day it didn't come. I tried to talk interns into buying one for us with my money, but no one had time. Then I tried to talk the nurses into letting me out to buy one at the vending machine which could be seen from the front door, but they couldn't do that. So we went the whole day without a newspaper. Little things like that could drive you nuttier than you were in the first place.

When it came time for my roommate to be discharged, she cried. She said she just couldn't make it on the outside. I asked her, "Can you make supper for your boyfriend?" She said, "Yes." I said, "Can you go to the grocery store and buy food?" She said, "Yes." I said, "Can you keep the house clean?" She said, "Yes." I said, "Well, you don't have to be President of the United States, you just have to be able to handle those sorts of things." She immediately brightened up and packed to go home. I guess she just needed someone to explain it to her that way.

After a few days, I was able to try Tegretol and within a week I was feeling better. I was stabilizing and soon felt better than I ever had. I was able to take things in stride and felt more in control of myself than I ever had. I felt like someone had given me the key to let me out of hell. No longer did I have to think about suicide all the time. My

126

moods didn't plunge me into the depths to raise me to heights. I felt "normal." Dr. Shupe agreed that the drug was working and that it seemed to be the solution for me. However, I asked him if he would try me on another hormone replacement therapy and this one made me even sicker than previous ones I tried. My blood pressure shot up to 150 over 100 and not only did I get a migraine, but I also threw up constantly. This meant that I couldn't leave the hospital until those problems were straightened out. But I was happier than I had ever been and felt that I could handle my life for the first time.

The other patients had friends and family who visited every night, but I had no family in town and the only friends who knew I was in the hospital were Shirley and Karen, who could visit only on the weekends. Dr. Shupe challenged me to prove to him that people cared about me, so I got my parents to come down for an interview. I never found out what was said, but I'll bet it was interesting. They never mentioned to me or to anyone else that they had found me in a locked psychiatric ward. It was as if it never happened.

I made friends with a middle-aged man, Bob, who was depressed and an alcoholic. To add to his problems, his wife decided to leave him while he was in the hospital. We spent time together on breaks, worked the newspaper's crossword together each morning, and teased each other that he would come and get in my bed at night to panic the nurses, who were beginning to worry that we were starting an inappropriate relationship. One thing he did do for me that was inappropriate -- I had a pair of scrubs that were comfortable and decent for me to wear in the evenings during visiting hours, but the elastic broke and I had to walk around holding them up. The nurses would not give me a safety pin for fear I would hurt myself with it, but he smuggled one in to me after his weekend leave. It was most appreciated. I wasn't allowed weekend leaves because my migraines had kept me from some of the activities and I had been dubbed "uncooperative."

Bob was a MASH sergeant in the Army, and we were right next to the helipad where the helicopters landed with emergencies. One of our major diversions was watching them land. I asked Bob why they were so slow and deliberate with the patients, while in the TV show "MASH" they always grabbed the stretchers and ran with the patients.

He laughed, and explained that in those cases there was usually one or more helicopters above waiting to land. "Oh."

At his request, I went to an AA meeting with him, and found that I did not like the touchy-feely atmosphere of the meeting at all. He needed my moral support, though, and I attended when he wanted me too and when my schedule allowed. I also went to a Bipolar Support Group, which should have been helpful, but wasn't. A man there told me I was an "idiot" for going to Parkland -- I should have hitchhiked to Maryland to go to the National Institutes of Health Hospital there. I also had problems with myself. I was sure now that I had medication that stabilized me that I didn't need anything else. I wanted to live my life as if I didn't have an illness. Again, I wasn't like those people in the support group; I had it all together and didn't need their help.

My blood pressure began to go down and it was looking as if I were going to get out, so Dr. Shupe sent me to the dental clinic to make sure I didn't have any issues there. He knew I didn't have any income at all -- I had already been assured by a social worker that the County was going to take care of my bill -- so he wanted to take care of any health problems I had. Talk about a doctor who cared about his patient; this was new to me.

Before I left, I met Michael, who was more of a "classic" manic-depressive. Michael was horribly depressed, thin with unkempt hair. He lay in a fetal position, explaining that this had happened to him before and that lithium would put him right. That was his condition when I left the hospital, so I didn't even recognize him when I ran into him at a luncheonette downtown a couple of months later. He was dressed in a suit, confident-looking with a sharp haircut and he had to remind me of where I met him. I said, "Well, I guess the lithium did it for you." He said, "Oh, yes, it always works." I asked him how much he was taking, and he replied that he stopped taking it because he felt so good. I had read that so often bipolar patients quit taking their medication when they start to feel better, but the contrast was so great in my mind between what he looked like in the hospital and what he looked like now that I made it a point to call the chaplain at the hospital to tell him the situation. I don't know whether he got back on his medication or not. Probably not. I knew that now that I was on a medication that was working that I would not stop taking it. I felt stable and better than I had ever felt before; you wouldn't catch me going off my meds.

After a month in the hospital, the time spent primarily, as I said, because of physical problems, I was released. I felt that I had a whole new life ahead of me and that I could handle anything now. Dr. Jim Shupe went on to become one of the most respected diagnosticians in the city, and is now a forensic psychiatrist practicing in Dallas. I was lucky to have been treated by him. One of the most important things about him was the fact that he was able to listen and give credence to my complaints. I hope he learned something from treating me, but he seemed to have it all under control even as a resident.

Years later, I had a friend, Karen, who was a psychiatric aide in a hospital in Dallas. She kept raving about a doctor she worked with who always seemed to sort of instinctively know what medications to prescribe for the patients. One day she said, "You know, that Dr. Shupe, he can just look at a patient and know what that person needs." I knew what she meant.

Going to the hospital was not a brilliant move on my part, but an action born of desperation. It was just like when I automatically called the mental health center in Norman. I instinctively did what I needed to do to save my life. It was pure luck that landed me in the best place for me in the city.

CHAPTER 28: Just Me

I knew the hole in my resume from being in the hospital did not look good, so I asked an attorney friend if I could say I worked in his office during that period. When he heard I had recently finished paralegal school, he did me one better. On the spot he offered me a "training" position. I would receive minimum wage, working eight hours a day for both him and his partner. I soon found out that the work, while not difficult, was harder than expected. The two attorneys had entirely different styles, with one expecting me at work at 8:30 a.m. and the other expecting me to stay until 7 p.m. I had a 45-minute bus ride each way so it made for a long day. I had also gone on a strict diet as soon as I went off antidepressants, and was able to take off thirty pounds and keep it off as long as I took Tegretol.

I set matters for hearing, handled correspondence, made copies, and mailed said copies. The work was not onerous, and I did learn some paralegal work, but the hours and the differing styles of the lawyers meant I had to juggle a lot. I was, however, able to pay my rent and my basic bills, so it was a tremendous help.

I worked for the two lawyers for five months in 1989, then went on to work for another legal firm in early 1990, this time for much more money. However, this time the atmosphere was strange. I put up with constant sexual harassment from my supervisor for months since every one else seemed to do so. (This was pre-Anita Hill.) I finally got tired of it and reported it to my supervisor, asking her to tell the supervisor to take down his Playboy pinups and to stop making suggestive remarks to me and to the other women there. I was fired the next day. I didn't even think of suing. I didn't think that suing a law firm was a bright idea.

I went back to work as a legal assistant temporary, and was able now to hold onto jobs. I was able to make fairly good money as a temporary, and to work regularly. I wanted a regular job and benefits, but with temporary work I was able to pay the bills. At one time I worked in downtown Dallas on the graveyard shift. It was the only time I ever worked that shift, and I felt more empathy for my father. I hated my upside-down life, and was glad when that job ended after only a few months.

Over the years I had noticed a job that was regularly advertised for a research assistant for a publisher in Dallas. I had applied for the position several times, and now, with an MA in history and a paralegal certificate, I landed it. I wondered why it had been advertised so many times, and worried about turnover, but I needed the job and took it in August of 1991.

You could cut the tension with a knife. It didn't take me long to find that the turnover problem wasn't that people hated the job, but that employees were fired on a regular basis. The turnover rate was 100 percent per year, because some people lasted only a matter of weeks. The working conditions were incredible, with the tension and the volume of work to be done. Kelly, a young paralegal, and I worked in the research center, taking dozens of calls a day and researching questions from customers. The job itself was great, doing research in my field, but the owner of the company was senile and took his cues from the President, who was a textbook case of paranoid personality disorder. She was convinced that the employees were plotting against both her and the company, which would have been rather counterproductive. She wore tennis shoes so she could sneak around and hear everything that was said. She often just made up things that we were supposed to have said about the job or the boss. I loved the job and needed the work, so just hunkered down and figured it would last as long as it would last. At least, since they fired everyone, I'd have unemployment and some time to look for another job when it was over.

I watched as colleague after colleague was fired, often for reasons that were totally obscure to me. After one such firing, they suddenly realized they had fired a writer they needed and asked me if I could take over his duties. Since it was definitely in my field and I had always wanted to write but didn't have any formal experience, I jumped at the chance. Of course, I got no extra pay and often had to do the work on my own time since I had to keep up my regular workload, but the experience was great. I wrote a monthly column on Supreme Court decisions, and once caught a mistake in a decision that was missed by everyone at the Court and the other Court watchers, including the guy at the *New York Times*. That was the high point of my career with the company.

This job did not offer insurance benefits, just a small stipend to help with private insurance. I asked my doctor at County about private insurance, because I had never had to deal with it before. He said, "Just be sure to tell them you are manic-depressive." It seemed reasonable, because it was a pre-existing condition so they wouldn't be responsible for it right away, and I knew there was a Texas law that required insurers not to discriminate against people with mental illnesses. So I was surprised to be turned down by the first company I applied with, and the second, and the third. They came out and said they were turning me down because I had bipolar disorder. When I called and pointed out to them that they were violating the law, I got, "We don't care about the law, we are not going to insure you." As a last resort I asked a Mensa friend who was an insurance agent to go to bat for me. He reported back to me that his company, a national, well-known company, would not insure me because "they are afraid that you will try to commit suicide, fail, and then they will have to pay for it." I pointed the law out to him, and he said his hands were tied.

I called the Texas Attorney General, who told me this was a common problem, and asked me to allow the state to file a test case in my name. Of course, if it were known at my job that I had bipolar disorder, I wouldn't last a day. I regretfully turned him down, and he said that's why they hadn't been able to enforce the law -- no one was able to go to court on it. Then I did what I should have done in the first place; I lied on the form, said I had never had a mental illness and got insurance right away. It is just another example of the discrimination against those with mental illnesses and it seems that no one is able to protect you -- not even the law.

We workers felt we were in a foxhole together and I made some good friends. The problem was that I never knew on a Monday morning who would be coming back to work. After I had been there for two years, I knew my time was limited because I did not receive the yearly merit raise even though I had set a longevity record for holding that position, and Kelly was fired about that time. But I had no clue when or why I would be terminated. It was always a surprise, always on Friday afternoon, and no one could ever expect it. Meanwhile, they were hiring contract writers for a special project. My current boyfriend was a well-known writer in Mensa, and Bailey needed work. I told the guy doing the hiring who Bailey was, and he hired him to do some articles.

Three weeks later, two weeks before Christmas, I was called into the boss' office on a Friday afternoon. By this time, I knew the pattern. They told me that "You are not working out." This was the only reason they gave me for firing me after two and a half years in the position. I knew there was no reason to press for a better reason or to ask for a reference. I just left.

The man who was in charge of apportioning the article for the special project simply doubled the work he gave Bailey, knowing I would get the extra work, without saying a word to either of us. For several months, I continued to work for the company without the bosses realizing they were still paying me. It helped me out a lot while I looked for work.

CHAPTER 29: SINGING

It was June of 1994 and I nervously clutched my purse in the reception area of a training company near my home. They had a writing position open and I wanted it so much. I got through the interview and was able to offer my writing samples from my previous job, but it was embarrassing to have to ask them not to contact my previous employer. I had heard the president of the previous company answering calls from prospective employers and knew she wouldn't have anything good to say about me. Luckily, the interviewer, who would be my supervisior if I got the job, just said. "Well, if you worked for them for two and half years, you must have been doing a pretty good job." So I dodged that bullet. I went away hopeful that I would get the job that I really wanted. A couple of weeks later, I did. And it was to be the best job I ever had, and my last.

It was a company that had started modestly but had grown rapidly. The owner had the idea of training people by using videos and satellite, thus obviating the need for people to go to expensive and time-consuming seminars and training classes. The idea had taken off, and the company grew almost impossibly fast. In the healthcare division, we trained doctors, nurses, nurses aides, x-ray technicians, radiologists, simply the whole gamut of heathcare professionals. But healthcare professions required the use of printed material and tests for extension classes, and that's where my job fit in. We sometimes wrote the material, but in most cases simply edited the material as given to us by the professional who would present the subject on camera. It was challenging and satisfying work.

As for my medication, I still went to the County for my prescriptions, but of course, since I was employed, paid full price. The attraction was that I could make appointments after working hours and that they simply gave me my Tegretol prescription with no argument. The conditions at the clinic were not improved, but it only took a few minutes every few months. I tried my best to forget that I was bipolar between appointments.

After working a couple of years, I decided to start using a private doctor. I simply picked the closest one out of the Yellow Pages. He was happy to supply me with my medication, but I soon found him to be cold and not helpful. At one point I ran out of pills about four days before my next appointment. I called his office to get medication to last me until the next appointment, but when the nurse called him for a refill, he said, "No, I don't know her. I won't give her a refill." The nurse was holding my records in her hands, so she called in the medication for me. I was not impressed by his attitude or his care, but I didn't worry because I knew what medication I needed and he was giving it to me. This turned out to be an error. You should always have a doctor you can count on, because you never know when you will need him.

The atmosphere at work was laid-back and casual, with employees setting their own hours and their own dress code. The idea was that you knew how much you needed to do and what you needed to look like to get your job done. My job generally required about fifty hours a week to get done, but I didn't complain. We had two deadlines a month to meet, and sometimes the work was hectic. I loved the work and the way I was treated, by clients, coworkers, and my bosses. I was also reassured by the fact that there was a large component of disabled people working there. The pay was not high, by any means, but I was able to pay my bills. I loved being able to write and edit for a living, and enjoyed being treated as an adult. One of the perks was working with the first runner-up to Miss America, finding out she was dumb as a box of rocks, and when she wasn't fixed up, she looked like anyone else.

In 1998, my mother finally succumbed to Alzheimer's Disease. It had been a trial taking care of her, because my father had been in denial and had not let us know how bad it had progressed. We didn't know her condition until the police ordered him to place her in a home after another search for her when she got lost. We had no idea she was wandering off or even that she was ill. He finally called and admitted the situation, leaving it to us to find a place for her. We did, then watched as she lost the ability to recognize her surroundings and us. It was quite painful and we were to the point where we were afraid we would have to do battle with my father over the insertion of a feeding tube. (She would never have wanted that; she had made her feelings to us quite clear over the years. Since her mother had died of the disease, we had often discussed it.) She died, suddenly, of a stroke.

At one point I called the nursing home and was told, to my horror, that my father had slapped a nurse's aide in a fit of frustration. She had declined to press charges or to sue because she knew how disturbed he was. The nursing home supervisor said, "You know, your father complains constantly that none of his children live within a hundred miles of him. After getting to know him, I know why you don't. None of you *can* live close to him." At that time my parents lived in a suburb of Oklahoma City, and my youngest sister lived in northern Oklahoma. I lived in Dallas, my younger sister in Austin, my brother in San Antonio, and my oldest sister in Houston. We were close enough to visit and to help in a crisis, but indeed, all of us had kept our distance. I hadn't even consciously thought of it before, but it was sad that we had to live so far from our mother, who we were all crazy about, to avoid our father's wrath.

Watching a vital, intelligent person die of this disease is one of the most painful things a spouse or child can endure. It takes away the identity and the dignity of the person and leaves nothing but a shell. My mother had suffered through it with her mother, placing her in a nursing home but caring for her until the end and she had left explicit instructions as to her care if she should develop the illness. However, my father could not accept her decline and insisted that she was much better than she was. He was prostrated by her death.

For some reason, he insisted on selling their home immediately after she died and my younger sister found him assisted living in her town. He was never happy there, and finding himself unable to face the first-year anniversary of her death, he simply died. To our surprise, he left each of us enough money to make a change in our lives. Well, actually, he left money to four of us. He was unhappy with the baby of the family, the one who had taken care of him the last year of his life, because he said she was only after his money. We threw the inheritance in one pot and divided it five ways so we would each get an equal amount. We had all suffered equally, but she had done something that the rest of us hadn't been able to do; she had taken care of him in his last days.

CHAPTER 30: THERE ARE MONSTERS

I couldn't believe it. I found my house. After one afternoon of looking, I found the house I wanted only a few blocks from my job. It was in a quiet neighborhood, on a quiet, tree-lined block that reminded me of the street I grew up on in Oklahoma City. It was the end of 1998, and I had a chance to own my own home for the first time since I was single. I wasn't sure about it, since it looked pretty raggedy on the inside, so I got my younger sister to drive up from Austin in a driving rainstorm to check it out. She had a real estate license and is a world-class decorator, and she assured me that it was a great deal and that we could do wonders with it.

So, I took the plunge and over the Christmas holidays my sister and I painted and papered and with my handyman turned an ugly duckling into a cozy swan. It had a huge living room for entertaining my Mensa friends, a small kitchen (fine for someone who didn't cook much) and a study, two bedrooms, and two baths. I was thrilled with it and with my good luck at finding it. I was never happier.

At work I had received a $10,000 raise and thanks from my boss for carrying us during a time when the three person unit only consisted of me and a new hire. It was rough but I had done the best I could and certainly felt rewarded. However, the company had been sold to a much larger company headquartered in New York and reorganizations came with a vengeance. I was put in a different division and got new bosses. Other than that, my job didn't change and everything went on as before.

But, shortly after I got my house, I noticed a rash on my body. I also began to get unexplained headaches. I knew better than to blow off the rash. A rare side effect of Tegretol, and one of the reasons it is not

139

used as much as it used to be, is Stevens-Johnson syndrome. It is a full-body rash that causes the skin to simply slip off the body, leaving the victim with the same effects as a 100 percent third-degree burn. It is usually fatal, and those who survive must undergo years of suffering and rehabilitation.

After a couple of days, I worked up the courage to call my doctor. As I said earlier, I had never been really impressed with him, but I was not ready for his reaction to my problem. He said, simply, "Stop taking the Tegretol and go to a dermatologist." I told him that not taking Tegretol without another drug to take its place would be difficult, since I had a job to do and wanted to stay halfway sane. He replied, "Well, I can't help you. You'd better get to a dermatologist soon. And don't take any more Tegretol!" Then he hung up the phone.

This is why you shouldn't put up with a doctor you don't trust or feel comfortable with just because he is giving you the medication you need. You never know when you will have a special circumstance come up or an emergency and you will need a doctor you have a rapport with to handle the situation. I learned that the hard way. Things can go sideways rapidly and in a big way before you realize it.

I was left frightened and feeling alone. I didn't feel that a dermatologist was the person to consult, because if Tegretol was the problem, I needed a lot more help than a skin cream. Frantic, I pulled out the Yellow Pages again and found a doctor who could see me right away. This time I hooked up with a caring, intelligent physician in Rudy Molina, who listened to my story, decided I had developed an allergy to Tegretol and did need a medication change, but said he would try to make it as seamless as possible because he knew I would have to continue working.

Dr. Molina got me off Tegretol and onto Depakote rapidly. He thought Depakote would work well on me and it may have; I was just so consumed by the side effects that I don't know how well it worked. Depakote made me hungry. All the time. All I could think about was food and I ate constantly. It was so bad that I woke up once or twice a night, so hungry I had to get out of bed and eat something. I stayed on the drug for six weeks to see if I would adjust to it, but I did not. The weight gain distressed me, but the main problem was that I couldn't concentrate on anything but food. We agreed that I would have to try something else.

It was about this time that a pharmaceutical company had come up with a new drug that they had hoped would be an effective treatment for bipolar disorder. When they tested it, they found it was not, but decided to market it to psychiatrists as a breakthrough for manic-depression because of the money that could be made. All this came out a couple of years later.

Unfortunately, the drug representative had presented his pitch to Dr. Molina, and he decided to try this new drug on me. A drug is usually tried on a patient for a period of about six weeks, because it may take time for the patient to get used to it and to its effects. As soon as I began taking the drug, I was skeptical. I stopped sleeping. I don't mean that I had trouble sleeping, I mean I stopped sleeping. I would get tired around 10 p.m. and go to bed, but would wake up at midnight and be completely unable to go back to sleep. I watched TV, read, and wrote stories, but nothing made me sleepy and I went to work each day after only two hours sleep. I also started losing it at work over small stuff. I did not feel that the drug was having any effect on me at all. After a couple of weeks, I started drinking wine at bedtime in an attempt to go to sleep. That didn't help either. It just made me more fuzzy-headed.

I told Dr. Molina that the drug wasn't helping, and he counseled patience. After a month of this, I knew things were going downhill rapidly. My new boss was a registered nurse and seemed to be a compassionate person; I thought perhaps telling her that truth would be wiser than letting things descend into chaos. I requested a meeting with her and explained why I wasn't sleeping at night, why I was coming to work looking like something the cat dragged into the office, and why I had a tendency to blow up over nothing. I said, "I have bipolar disorder, I can't really control my moods." I could see in her eyes that I had made a mistake. I knew then that I never should have admitted that I had bipolar disorder, but it was too late to take it back. I requested a meeting with a vice president and told him my problems; he said he would work with me. Two weeks later, I had my yearly review and the word "fire" was used. I was also told not to talk with that particular vice president again. This did not bode well.

This started the hardest year of my life. While it was obvious that my boss had made up her mind to get rid of me, I had worked for another vice-president of the company for six years. She was still head of my division and I thought perhaps she would not want to let me go. Why, it was only the year before that I had won an award for being such a good employee.

However, now my assignments kept changing and in consequence I made mistakes, which were always written up. If I made a good save, such as the time I caught an article saying just the opposite of what it should have said just before we went to print, nothing was said. I stayed in denial, not believing that I would lose the job I loved and that I thought I was good at, because I was bipolar. I somehow completely denied the reality that was right in front of me.

At one point I was suffering greatly from spring allergies, which were not helped by a field of several acres of wildflowers next to the office. I told my boss that I was going home sick, but she asked me to wait until after the staff meeting. I was full of allergy pills and could hardly stay awake for the meeting, but since my supervisor usually wrote up an outline of the meeting for us, I wasn't too worried. However, this time, at the end of the meeting, she turned to me and said, "Jane, please write up the meeting for the staff." Of course, I was completely unable to and was written up for my failure.

I asked permission to work from home while my medications were changed so I would not rub people the wrong way. I was told that was impossible. Later, a member of my unit moved to Florida and was allowed to work from there, so I could only conclude that the purpose was to keep me on the job so I could mess up. There were several humiliating meetings in which I was forced to discuss the progress of my medication stabilization with the head of human resources, the vice president, and my two bosses. All were written up for my personnel file.

One thing that had always been a problem was that my concentration problems had made me a poor proofreader. Since there were three in the unit, the others helped me by doing more proofing while I made up for that lack with extra writing. Now, though, I had to become a good proofer. This was impossible for me, and, three weeks after my vice president was reassigned, I was fired on May 3 of 2001. That night Anita, a good friend, came over, listened to me and fed me popcorn. At 6 a.m. the next morning Penny, my neighbor and steadfast friend, drove me to work and helped me clean out the office I had occupied for seven years. I was given three months' severance pay and, after that, would be on my own at the age of 55.

CHAPTER 31: THERE ARE ANGELS

I took an inventory of what I had. A Masters degree, a house that I loved, experience in teaching, social work, and writing. Most importantly, Dr. Molina had managed, when he realized that the new drug was simply not going to work, to put together a combination of three drugs, Paxil, Respiradol, and Topamax, which were almost as effective as Tegretol and had no side effects. I also had a terribly deflated ego, a feeling that I had failed at something where I desperately wanted to succeed. Dr. Molina's nurse told me I was not alone. They had another bipolar patient at my job who was going through the same thing I had just traversed; so I guess it wasn't personal.

After the information about the drug became public, I spoke with a lawyer who was engaged in a class-action suit against the pharmaceutical company. She told me that she had heard my story over and over, that many people on the drug had felt it necessary to tell their employers that they were bipolar to explain their odd behavior, and were then fired for it. At the end, they decided to limit the suit to those who tried, or did, commit suicide while on the drug.

I didn't attempt suicide, but was suicidal all during the time I was on the drug. I was unable to read or listen to music or to sleep. I had spent most of the time I was on the drug pacing and waiting for time to pass. I had something to keep me going, though. When I moved into my new home, I had gone through some old photos and found my pictures of the Four Preps, taken forty years before. That same week, the movie they were in played on TV and it made me wonder what had happened to them. I found a website for their lead singer, Bruce Belland, and we started corresponding. His warmth came through on his e-mails as he caught me up on my old friends' lives, letting me know that both Ed and Marv had died just the year before, and that

Glen had become a successful TV producer, but that he, Bruce, was still in a singing group. We traded e-mails about politics and philosophy and rekindled our friendship. It was a big part of what kept me going during a dark period of my life. Anticipating Bruce's e-mails gave me something to live for and were a pleasant distraction during a time when all I could do was pace from room to room and suicidal ideation and mood changes were hitting me like a sledgehammer. He doesn't realize it, but he may have saved my life during this dark period.

My Mensa friends were also supportive, and many of them were unemployed at the time. It was just a bad time to be out of a job, but I tried hard to find employment. Being older didn't help. Also, the sneaking suspicion that if I couldn't hold the last job meant that I couldn't get or hold another, didn't help either. But I must have applied for 200 jobs. I got eleven interviews, but didn't get past the first screening one each time. I desperately tried everything I could think of to find work in all fields that I had experience in.

Meanwhile, my money was running out. I had some savings, mostly thanks to a $20,000 win in the lottery about a year before I was fired. I kept $14,000 after taxes, and spent about half of that for furniture. The rest I saved. I also had about $10,000 in a 401K. I got unemployment for a year, but was not eligible for extended benefits. I spent as little as I could, and also took a couple of temporary jobs. I was fired from both of them. There were extenuating circumstances, but that didn't make me feel any better.

My first reaction was to feel that I would kill myself before I would give up my house, but soon sanity prevailed and I realized that losing a house was not the worst thing that could happen. Indeed, during that period, foreclosures were at a high and many people were losing their homes. I would just have to do the best I could and hope for the best. This is where the effect of medication shows itself. If I had not been on medication, I may very well have committed suicide over the loss of my job and my house. The medication allowed me to remain stable and to keep things in perspective.

By 2003, I realized I was not going to find a job and I was not going to save my house. I had spent everything I had and still, in my heart, believed I wasn't really capable of working. The experience of being fired from the best job I ever had broke my spirit. That's when I realized that I would have to apply for Social Security Disability. In the past I had believed that was giving up, that you had to keep trying. But now I knew I had reached the point where trying wasn't going to get me there any more, that I had to admit that I was finally too ill to work. It was discouraging, but I was willing to try.

I put my home on the market and sold it after only a week, thanks in great part to the decorating my sister had done. I made a good profit on the sale, which would allow me to live while I applied for Social Security. My doctor recommended that I hire a lawyer and that I move to a county that spent more on mental health than Dallas County. I did both, and started the long wait that it takes to apply for disability. I moved from Dallas after living there for over thirty years. It was scary, not doing anything but waiting, but after sixteen months I finally had a hearing. Both my attorney and I were surprised to find that after studying my doctor's statements and my employment records, the hearing judge had determined that I was disabled even before the hearing started.

I was awarded a small monthly check and now have a steady income that I can count on. I live in a tiny Texas town, but one which is close to a good community mental health center. The doctor who worked with me when I moved here was Stuart Crane, who helped me with obtaining my benefits and understood my terror at changing my medication once again, so he helped me continue on my current medication even though the state did not want to pay for such an expensive drug. Dr. Kerrie Halfant has also worked with me, helping me adjust to a life without work.

I struggled all my adult life with working at a job when I had one, finding one when I didn't have one, and keeping one. Often there were extenuating circumstances, and I often held a job by dint of purely working hard, but my illness often caused me to lose jobs or not be able to find one. Stress was always difficult for me, and, for example, the stress of two print deadlines a month, as I had at my last position, kept me upset much of the time. I also clashed with co-workers but usually got along well with supervisors. When I didn't, of course, I would soon lose a job, no matter how hard I tried. I was often without work, and when I was sickest, couldn't find or hold even temporary jobs. This left me unable to plan or save for retirement, as I was usually scrambling to pay my current bills. I would have loved to have settled down in my last job and held it until retirement age, but that was not to be.

After I learned that I was manic-depressive, I was glad that I did not have the symptom that so many have, the one that sends people with bipolar disorder on spending sprees, which often leaves them in incredible debt or bankruptcy. I have no explanation as to why that particular symptom was not part of my illness, though I will admit I am not always as careful with money as I should be. I have read in other books how people with manic depression went on insane sprees, spending thousands of dollars on things they did not need, only to come down later and be faced with massive bills. I am sure that if that were part of my illness, I would have done the same, as the illness is not something that can be controlled with will power. My doctors can't give me an answer as to why I was spared this, either.

The symptoms that bothered me the most were the lack of judgment, the hyper sexuality, and the feelings of invulnerability that one gets with the highs, which cause a person to do incredibly stupid things that you have to pay for later; sometimes with the loss of friends who do not understand or who have given up on you, or by the loss of a job, or even a marriage. Of course, the depression is also awful -- the lows that cause suicidal feelings, feelings of worthlessness, of inability to accomplish anything. Both moods in me were accompanied with irritability, which did not help with my relationships.

Feeling normal with medication has been a great blessing and one that I would not give up. I am more creative, not less, on medication, and my life is less exciting and certainly more organized and stable on medication. The period of time that I had to go off medication, when I developed that allergy to my meds, convinced me that I will be happy to stay on medication for the rest of my life. I have never been a user of alcohol, and have given up any use of illegal drugs; neither mix well with my medication. After all, what you are doing with alcohol and drugs is trying to alter your brain chemistry. I have had enough alteration to last the rest of my life. My goal now is to stay clear-headed and stable.

I miss my Mensa friends in Dallas, but I write for Mensa publications, both local and national and keep in touch that way. I will never be completely "normal" but have tried to live life as normally as possible. Many times I have wondered what my life would have been like if I hadn't been born with bipolar disorder. Would I have gone to Washington, DC and become involved in politics, my first love? Would I have taken that police job, and become one of the first policewomen in the country? Would I have been a teacher all my life, as I planned as a young girl? Would I have had a good marriage? Everyone has disabilities to overcome, and I can live with the fact that I did the best I could with what I had. That's all any of us can do.

Besides, I know myself as I am. If I had not had bipolar disorder, I would have been someone else. I like who I am and what I have accomplished. I wouldn't be anyone else if I were given the choice. I know me, my capabilities, and my failings. I am comfortable with myself.

Thanks to Ralf Kittenbacher, Alpha Photography, for this photograph.

END WORD

If you have bipolar disorder, or if you have a loved one with the disorder, don't give up looking for that balance and stability that is possible. Don't let doctors tell you what works; listen to them, of course, try what they suggest and work with them, but when they tell you something works and it doesn't, move on to another doctor or another institution. You have the right to feel better. You have the right to stability, to get off that roller coaster that controls you. But, only you can do it. Nobody else can do it for you. Nurses, doctors, therapists can help, but they can't give you the motivation to keep working, to keep trying, to keep demanding the care you need to find that key that will let you out of hell. It's there, you just have to keep striving and reaching for it.

I know you have cried, I know you have felt desperate, I know that you feel like killing yourself to make the pain stop. But it doesn't have to be like that. You can smile, you can feel peaceful, you can feel like living. Believe me, it is all possible. If you know it is possible, you can work towards it with the knowledge that there is light at the end of the dark tunnel you are in. I've been in that tunnel and I know how you feel. When I was reaching for the peace of stability, I wasn't even sure I could reach it. I just knew I couldn't continue the way I was, and I didn't want to die. Doctors and nurses encouraged me to keep trying and my will to live made me believe that there was something better for me.

I was able to work for years without people knowing that I had a mental illness after I found the right medication. It was only the allergy that I developed to Tegretol that outed me. Employers and others have a great fear that persons with bipolar disorder will go postal at any time. We all must work to eradicate this stigma. People with bipolar disorder are much more likely to commit suicide than they are to hurt others. Suicide is a real danger for those with the illness; it is when we lose hope that things will ever improve in our life that we give up. Don't ever give up. Keep trying. There is always something more to try; another medication, another therapy. My life completely turned around. I've seen others' lives turned around by the right medications and the right therapies. You don't have to be left out. There are community mental health centers if you cannot afford private mental health care. Go to the hospital, like I did, if you need to. Make them listen to you. Don't be aggressive, but be assertive. It is worth it. You are worth it.

People with bipolar disorder often have to try many different medications to find the right one or the right combination. There is no one medication that works for everyone; just as everyone manifests the disease in different ways, everyone's body chemistry is a little different, and, unfortunately, the only way to find the right medication is by trial and error. This can be extremely frustrating but think of it as adventures in pharmacology. You are Alice in Wonderland wondering, "Hey, I wonder what this one will do?" And keep trying. You will find that key to let you our of hell. And that is worth it.

While people with depression will find their depression lifting after a time even if they do nothing, bipolar disorder cannot be controlled except with medication, and it is a lifelong commitment to take medication. As soon as the depression lifts, we are thrown into mania, which is perhaps not as unpleasant, but can have unpleasant consequences. Then, back to depression. It makes sense that groups like Scientologists, cults, do not want their members to take medications for psychiatric illnesses, for they often depend on brainwashing to keep their members compliant. And brainwashing is simply an induced depression.

Try to live as though you have a disease like diabetes. You have to know what you are dealing with; you have to monitor yourself and keep up with any changes in your illness. Everybody has something to deal with, we just got bipolar disorder. Sometimes I don't sleep, sometimes I get a little manic, but I watch myself and try to keep myself on an even keel. Pay attention -- are you sleeping? Are you pacing? Do you lose your focus? Are your medications making you feel peaceful and stable? Or do you feel out of control and irritable? Are you blowing things out of proportion? Seek the peaceful, self-confident, and stable. Perhaps your meds need to be changed or its time to change doctors.

Nothing about bipolar disorder is easy. It's not easy living with the roller coaster ups and downs of the illness, the diagnosis is not easy, and it's not easy finding the right medication. You have to stay on your medication, monitor yourself, and stay under a doctor's care for the rest of your life. Some people seem to feel that if they could just find that magic bullet, everything would come together and they wouldn't have to fight for their stability. But, there is no amino acid therapy, no nutritional therapy, no magic. It is a lifelong fight and you can never give up.

I have heard so many with bipolar disorder say that they "don't want to be on pills for the rest of their lives." I can't figure that one out. I would so much rather take a couple of pills a day than deal with mood swings, depression, irritability, inability to get along with others, mania, desperation, and all the other symptoms of bipolar disorder. And that part is easy. You just take a pill. Any fool can do that. Once you've found the right pill or the right combination of drugs.

Count on your friends, count on your family, and if you don't have their support, make your own by joining support groups and message boards. Learn as much as you can about the illness by researching it at the library or on the web. But mostly, count on yourself. You can do it. I know it sometimes seems impossible, but the key is within your grasp. You just have to reach for it.

APPENDIX

THINGS I HAVE LEARNED...

- People are not pleased or intrigued when you get in touch with them after years of being out of communication. They probably remember you from a manic or depressed state and don't particularly want to go through it with you again.

- Don't continue with a doctor or dentist who seems to have a problem with your illness. Bipolar disorder will color your whole relationship with this healthcare provider, and he will not be able to treat or diagnose you properly.

- The doctor does not decide when your medication is right. You do. The proper medication fits you. It feels like a key slipping into a lock. On the other hand, no medication is perfect. You have to decide what side effects you can tolerate.

- Go to a psychiatrist. A medical doctor may have your best interests in mind, but he or she is not up on the latest mental health medications. They are coming out with new ones constantly. The ones I started on are not even being prescribed now.

- You always have options. There are community clinics everywhere. You may have to wait, but they have to see you. If you live in a state where mental health is not a priority, you may actually want to move to a place where more is spent on it. You may have to scrape up the money to go to a private doctor for diagnosis, and continue with a clinic when you find the proper medication.

155

- Mentally ill people are the most-discriminated against people in America today. Who else has special provisions in health insurance that only pays half of their care? You have to take care of yourself.

- Always make certain that every important interaction you have with a healthcare worker is properly documented. Use a tape recorder if you are worried. Your word is simply never taken. You are the crazy one.

- Be persistent. Especially with public mental health centers. You are just another person they have to care for. If you are not happy with your care, ask for a supervisor. You do not have to stay with the doctor you have been assigned to; you have the right to ask for another if you do not feel you are getting proper care.

- Bipolar disorder is not easily diagnosed. When it is diagnosed, it is not easy to find the proper medication. Lithium works for many, but not for all. It takes both patience and persistence. I was diagnosed in 1983 and did not find the right medication until 1988. Don't give up.

- Bipolar disorder is often confused with substance abuse. So many people with the disorder self-treat with illegal substances that it often confuses the matter. Are you taking illegal drugs to moderate your moods? Stop. It doesn't work and actually makes things worse.

- Never let your employer know you are bipolar. Most people are afraid of the disorder and have prejudices against those who have it. On the other hand, do tell your best friends and, of course, significant others. You need the support. I only lost one "friend" by telling her and, of course, decided she wasn't much of a friend. Those I told were otherwise unfailingly supportive.

- Explain it to people by telling them it is an illness like diabetes. Those with diabetes can't control their blood sugar and must take medication to control it; you can't control your moods and must take medication to help you control them.

- Regular sleep is all-important. Your doctor will help you to regulate your sleep; missing sleep may throw you into a manic state or deepen your depression. I take melatonin to help me go to sleep and sometimes I take generic non-prescription sleep aids. I have always had trouble going to sleep. Regularity in meals also will help regulate your moods. Get yourself on a schedule.

- Just because you don't have all the symptoms does not mean you are not bipolar. One of the more common symptoms and one that is always associated with bipolar disorder is spending sprees. I never really had that problem. I might buy a CD that I didn't really need or four lipsticks when I needed one, but I never spent myself into debt. Doesn't mean I wasn't bipolar. I just didn't have that particular symptom.

- People with bipolar disorder are often creative and sometimes avoid treatment because they fear it will stifle creativity. This is not true. I could never get it together to write before I had treatment because my thinking was too chaotic. If you read about individuals with bipolar disorder, many say they found their creativity more channeled and easier to manage after treatment.

- Join a support group if you feel the need. People there will understand your problems and offer help.

- Help your doctor understand your feelings by mirroring how you feel by how you look. Don't wear makeup and fix your hair if you feel rotten. (If you're a man, don't shave or press your clothes). Letting him or her see how you feel helps the doctor understand how you feel. Conversely, if you feel good, show it in the way you look.

- Do work with a doctor you feel comfortable with and you trust. While things may be going well now, you never know when an emergency is waiting around the corner. You don't want a doctor you don't feel comfortable with managing a crisis.

- One of the best pieces of advice I ever got was from a caseworker. If you feel yourself slipping into mania or depression, distract yourself.

Don't sit around and obsess. Cook something, go for a walk, clean out the closet. It works.

- Being aggressive, raising your voice, or screaming and shouting, does not work

- Being assertive, asking for rights, demanding that you be listened to, does work.

- I take my nighttime medications a couple of hours before bedtime. That way the meds have time to start working before I actually go to bed, so I am ready for sleep when I do go to bed.

- When you are searching for that right combination of meds, keep a journal of your feelings and actions for the doctor. As your moods change, you may forget how you feel or what you did. When you go to your appointment, you will have something concrete to tell the doctor. This will help him/her know how you've been feeling and acting.

- If you feel alone, there are message boards for people with bipolar disorder. Dr. Phil, for example, has one. Here you can find support from people with the same problems as you have.

BIPOLAR DISORDERS

"Bipolar disorders include Bipolar I, Bipolar II Disorders and others. These simply mean that depression and manic or hypománic states alternate with each other in an individual. Features associated with bipolar disorders are suicide, child abuse, spousal abuse, or violent behavior which may occur during severe mania or those with psychotic features. Other features include school truancy or failure, workplace failure, divorce, eating disorders, attention-deficit/hyperactivity disorder, panic disorder, social phobia, and substance abuse.

Bipolar disorder is often misdiagnosed and even after diagnosis the proper medication may be difficult to determine. There are no laboratory tests to distinguish bipolar disorder from depression. Bipolar disorder, unlike depression, is as equally common in men as in women. Some women have their first episode in the postpartum period, and those with Bipolar I disorder have an increased risk of developing subsequent episodes, often psychotic, during the postpartum period.

Intervals between episodes tends to decrease as a person ages. Changes dues to sleep-wake cycle such as time zone changes or sleep deprivation may precipitate or worsen an episode."

Depressive Episode
"A major depressive episode is a period of at least two weeks during which there is either a depressed mood or the loss of interest or pleasure in nearly all activities. The individual must also experience at least four other symptoms that include:

• Changes in appetite or weight, sleep and psychomotor activity

- Decreased energy

- Feelings of worthlessness or guilt

- Difficulty thinking, concentrating, or making decisions

- Recurrent thoughts of death or suicidal ideation, plans, or attempts

The episode must be accompanied by clinically significant distress or impairment in social, work, or other important areas of functioning. Many individuals report or show increased irritability. Loss of interest is nearly always present. Appetite is usually reduced, though some may have increased appetite and crave specific foods. There may be a significant gain or loss in weight.

The most common sleep disturbance is insomnia. Individuals wake in the middle of the night and have difficulty returning to sleep, or wake too early and cannot return to sleep. Or, they cannot get to sleep at night. Less frequently, people oversleep.

Psychomotor changes include agitation as in the inability to sit still, pacing, hand-wringing, or retardation, when the person has slowed speech or thinking. Decreased energy, fatigue, tiredness, and fatigue are common. Many individuals have impaired ability to think, concentrate, or make decisions, and may be unable to function at school or work.

There may be thoughts of death, suicide, or suicide attempts. These can range from transient thoughts of suicide to actual plans. Motivations may include a desire to give up in the face of insurmountable obstacles or to end a painful emotional state that seems endless."

Manic Episode

"A manic episode is a period in which there is an abnormally elevated, expansive, or irritable mood. The mood must be accompanied by at least three symptoms from a list that includes:

- Inflated self-esteem

- Decreased need for sleep

- Pressure of speech

- Flight of ideas

- Distractibility

- Increased involvement in goal-directed activities or psychomotor agitation

- Excessive involvement in pleasurable activities with a high potential for painful consequences

The manic episode mood may be described as euphoric, unusually good, cheerful, or high. It is characterized by unceasing and indiscriminate enthusiasm for interpersonal, sexual, or occupational interactions. However, the predominant mood disturbance may be irritability. The alternation between euphoria and irritability is often seen.

Inflated self-esteem may reach delusional proportions, from uncritical self-confidence to giving advice on matters on which a person has no knowledge to embarking on a project for which they have no ability. Grandiose delusions are common.

There is a decreased need for sleep. The person usually awakens hours early, or may even go for days without sleep. Manic speech is pressured, loud, rapid, and difficult to interrupt. Individuals may talk nonstop without regard for others' wishes. Speech may include complaints, hostile remarks, or angry tirades.

The individual's thoughts may race, often at a rate faster than can be articulated. This flight of ideas may be evidenced by a continuous flow of accelerated speech with abrupt changes from one topic to another. Distractibility is shown by an inability to screen out irrelevant stimuli. This may be evidenced by a reduced ability to differentiate between thoughts that are relevant to a topic and those that are not.

The increase in goal-directed activity often involves excessive planning of, and excessive participation in, multiple activities. Increased sexual drive and behavior are often present. Almost invariably there is increased sociability, such as renewing old acquaintances or calling friends at all hours of the day or night without regard to the intrusive and demanding nature of these interactions.

Individuals often display psychomotor agitation or restlessness by pacing or holding multiple conversations at the same time. Expansiveness, unwarranted optimism, grandiosity, and poor judgment often lead to an imprudent involvement in activities such as buying sprees, reckless driving, foolish business investments, and sexual behavior unusual for that person, even though these activities may have painful consequences.

Individuals with a manic disorder frequently do not recognize that they are ill and resist treatment. They may change their appearance, travel impulsively, gamble and engage in antisocial behaviors. Some individuals, especially those with psychotic features, may become physically assaultive or suicidal."[5]

---

[5] American Psychiatric Association. (1994). *Diagnostic and Statistical Manual of Mental Disorders.* pp. 320-323, 328-329, 350-353

SUGGESTED READINGS

There are dozens of books on the mood disorders, but here are just a few that I have found helpful.

Diagnostic and Statistical Manual of Mental Disorders. (1994) American Psychiatric Association. (4ᵗʰ ed.)

Duke, Patty. (1988). *Call Me Anna*. Bantam.

Duke, Patty, &Hochman, Gloria. (1992). *A Brilliant Madness: Living with Manic-Depressive Illness*. Bantam.

Fawcett, Jan, Golden, Bernard, and Rosenfeld, Nancy. (2000). *New Hope for People with Bipolar Disorder*. Three Rivers Press.

Fieve, Ronald. (1989.) *Moodswing: Dr. Fieve on Depression*. William Morrow & Co.

Jamison, Kay Redfield. (1996). *Touched with Fire: Manic-Depressive Illness and the Artistic Temperament*. Free Press.

Jamison, Kay Redfield. (1997). *An Unquiet Mind: A Memoir of Moods and Madness*. Vintage.

Mondimore, Francis Mark. (1999). *Bipolar Disorder: A Guide for Patients and Families*. The Johns Hopkins University Press.